Residential Interiors Today

EDITED BY CATHERINE C. CRANE

Residential Interiors Today

An Insider's View from *Residential Interiors* magazine

WHITNEY LIBRARY OF DESIGN,
an imprint of WATSON-GUPTILL PUBLICATIONS/NEW YORK

First published 1977 in New York by Whitney Library of Design,
an imprint of Watson-Guptill Publications,
a division of Billboard Publications, Inc.,
1515 Broadway, New York, N.Y. 10036

Library of Congress Cataloging in Publication Data
Main entry under title:
Residential interiors today.

Includes index.
1. Interior decoration—Addresses, essays, lectures.
I. Crane, Catherine C., 1940–
NK2125.R47   1977   729   77–23740
ISBN 0–8230–7443–9
ISBN 0–8230–7444–7 pbk.

Printed and bound by Amilcare Pizzi S.p.A., Milan, Italy

First Printing, 1977
Designed and produced in association with Chanticleer Press, Inc.,
New York, N.Y. 10017

Contents

Acknowledgments

Foremost thanks are due Don Carroll for conceiving the idea of *Residential Interiors Today*. He sensed the public's awareness and appetite for good interior design—and its confusion. As Publisher of *Interiors* (now *Contract Interiors*) and *Residential Interiors* magazines, two outstanding professional journals directed to practicing interior designers, he felt his staff could offer enlightening answers to the layman. He thought material from *Residential Interiors* magazine could be reinterpreted and redirected to explain the world of the professional designer to the curious consumer. Don Carroll's idea gave birth to this book. He deserves thanks for an idea whose time has come.

Deep appreciation is due to the editors of *Residential Interiors* for their initial selection of the material published. Richard W. Jones, the present Editor of the magazine, and C. Ray Smith, the previous Editor, are responsible for selecting the magazine's intriguing interiors. Editors who did the initial research and writing for the magazine's reports are owed a debt of gratitude. Besides Richard Jones and C. Ray Smith, they include Ruth Miller Fitzgibbons, Susan Szenasy, Roger Yee, Betty Raymond, Marian Page, Lois Wagner Green, Lois Hagen, and contributors Peter Carlsen, Ray Rhinehart, Robert Mehlman, Carol Frankel and Charles Kreibel. Harry Siegel is to be thanked for the inspiration from his book *A Guide to Business Principles and Practices for Interior Designers*.

We would like to express our appreciation to the following photographers: Peter Aaron, Gerald Allen, Jaime Ardiles-Arce, Jeremiah O. Bragstad, Thomas Brooks, Orlando Cabanban, Richard Champion, Christopher Danes, Bill Engdahl of Hedrich-Blessing, John Fulker, Alexandre Georges, Jack O. Hedrich of Hedrich-Blessing, Hickey-Robertson, Elyse Lewin, Taylor Lewis, Michelle Maier, Claude May, Norman McGrath, Robert Perron, Louis Reens, James V. Righter, Ed Stoecklein, Ezra Stoller, Rob Super, Masaru Suzuki, Fritz Taggart, Wayne Thom, Bob Van Noy.

I would like to extend my personal thanks to those who helped me with the rewriting. Without them I would have been a basket case. Richard Jones, the Editor of *Residential Interiors* magazine and a past President of the American Society of Interior Designers, offered advice and guidance on how to use a designer. I also was assisted in this regard by a speech by designer Emily Malino and a report by publicist Ola Pfeiffer. Besides her impressive initial market coverage, Susan Szenasy, Senior Editor, was enormously helpful in verifying information on new products and in checking out my reports. Ruth Miller Fitzgibbons, Managing Editor—I thank for her constant encouragement and occasional constructive criticism. Ruth Johnston, Assistant Production Manager, showed great good spirit and efficiency in gathering together all the photographic film. She and Nat Cullinan, my office pinwheel mates, I thank for being good sounding boards. I am appreciative of Robert Mehlman's expertise on antiques. Ben Marchetto, Production Manager of the magazine, was good for jokes and advice.

I would like to express my appreciation of the late Charles E. Whitney, founder of *Interiors* magazine, parent magazine to *Residential Interiors*. Formerly an editor on his staff, I am now pleased to have something to do with a book grouped in the Whitney Library of Design.

Residential Interiors and *Interiors* magazines are now published by Billboard Publications, Inc. This book is being published by another division of Billboard, Watson-Guptill Publications. I would like to thank Jules Perel, the leader of the Watson-Guptill division, for seeing the merits of this project. My editor Sarah Bodine deserves congratulations for her patience and good humor throughout. She certainly has earned my warm gratitude!

Chanticleer Press deserves recognition for the fine design of this book. Gudrun Buettner should be congratulated for making aesthetic coherence out of chaos, and Emma Staffelbach will soon be sainted for her patience in seeing through the details of production.

Amilcare Pizzi, S.p.A., Milan, Italy, is appreciated for the printing and binding of this book.

I wish to ask female designers for their forbearance. Throughout the text I have used the male personal pronoun instead of the combined forms of he/she, him/her. I'm all for women's lib, except for what it's doing to the language. It all gets so awkward! Please understand when I say "he" or "him," I am referring to either a male or female person.

Last and most important, I would like to thank the designers and manufacturers whose imagination, aesthetic intuition, and good solid common sense not only made this book possible, but inspired its creation.

Foreword

This is not intended as a picture book for your coffee table or as an escape for you to build your castle in Spain or as an invitation to live vicariously with the art or antique collection of some little-known millionaire or well-known celebrity. This is a reference book —a guide to good design. It should acquaint you with a broad selection of products and styles. It will tell you the reasons behind the fashion trends of the times. It will introduce you to a wide variety of interior design problems and show you designer solutions. It will help you find the look you like. It will unravel the mysteries of working with an interior designer.

We believe residential interior design should be personal. Your home should be designed *for* you, *for* your lifestyle, but not necessarily *by* you any more than you would rely on your own workmanship for the chair or automobile you buy or the appliance you use.

Interior design requires educated solutions to the use of space. Truly good design involves so much more than good taste, a flair for color and rearranging furniture. The professional designer must have a complete formal education and apprenticeship and a knowledge of the myriad designer products, the specialized forms and applications of fibers, fabrics, wallcovering, lighting, carpets and rugs, laminates, systems. He must keep up with the latest developments in a very dynamic field, ever-changing developments in design forms, functions, technology and social values. Don't confuse the professional with the mail-order or self-professed decorator.

We have been reporting the latest developments in design to the professional for nearly ninety years. It began in 1888 with a magazine called *The Upholsterer.* The magazine grew into *The Upholsterer and Interior Decorator,* developed into *The Interior Decorator,* and in 1940 was renamed *Interiors.* From covering the design and upholstery of a chair to reporting on the entire interior of an office or a hotel, the changes in the name of the magazine reflected the ever-widening scope of the services rendered by the professional designer. In 1974 *Interiors* introduced a quarterly residential design supplement for those designers specializing in homes. By January 1976 the quarterly had grown into an independent magazine called *Residential Interiors,* and now *Interiors* magazine has been renamed *Contract Interiors* to reflect the fact that it specializes in covering the design of public spaces—offices, hotels, restaurants, schools, hospitals—in general all interiors other than those in private homes.

When then, after ninety years of servicing the professional alone, should we introduce a publication and offer it for sale to the consumer? Simply because we felt that the consumer, the interior design student, and the professional designer alike would profit from a wide variety of designer interiors expressing very different design problems and solutions. Then, too, many of our professional subscribers told us it was about time we took this step. With the growth of the industry and the growing interest of the consumer, it was inevitable for us to serve as the communications link between the designer and the public.

Having long exposure and experience with the designer's world —his work, his sources, his problems, his view of his profession, and having enormous respect for the professional designer, we would like to share our insights with you and encourage you to rely upon the guidance of one of these professionals.

As the title of this publication suggests, the interiors as well as the products within these covers were introduced to professionals in the field through the pages of *Residential Interiors* and its predecessor, *Interiors Residential Quarterly.* All material has been rewritten for the consumer.

When this book was in its planning stage, we employed standard market research techniques and interviews with "focus" groups to determine attitudes toward designers. These interviews suggested that many people who could easily afford the slight additional cost for a designer were reluctant to hire one because they felt unprepared. "They know everything," one person told us, and "I know so very little." We want to do "our thing, not theirs," was another typical report.

Most people are not aware of how much designers influence their lives. We are frequently introduced to new fashions or trends in clothing by the designer. We don't always realize that the form and function of every package we buy, of most hotels and restaurants that we enjoy, and of virtually every office building or hospital which provides a better working or living environment is the art form of the designer. For the single most important environment in your life—your home—why should you depend entirely upon what limited experience you may have of style or products when there is plenty of professional help available at reasonable rates?

Professional designers *are* experts, but they are experts trained to please you—to find the unique combination for every individual —even the different personalities within your family. Whether you work with an independent professional designer, one associated with an architectural, interior design or product design firm, or one associated with a store or design studio doesn't matter, but don't design your home alone. Read every page of this book, become acquainted with the different design sources and styles, then call a designer. He will welcome *your* input, what *you* like and will help you to express *your* personality and solve *your* design problems.

I would especially like to thank the editor of *Residential Interiors Today,* Catherine C. Crane, for her careful selection of the work and sources from *Interiors Residential Quarterly* and *Residential Interiors* and for her design analysis and interpretation of this material.

In the long run, a better designed home will be a better place to live in—more functional, comfortable and beautiful—or simply more homey. For right now we hope that this book will help you to know a little more about the designer and good design, particularly about what might be especially good for you.

Donald J. Carroll
Publisher
Contract Interiors
Residential Interiors

INTRODUCTION
Trends of the Times

[handwritten margin note: Factors Influencing Interior Designers]

What are the trends in home furnishings? Contemporary styles are more popular, but then so are traditional styles. Interiors these days, more often than not, are an eclectic mixture of both contemporary and traditional styles.

Home furnishings are more comfortable, sensuous, voluptuous than before, but they are also more movable, space-saving and easy-care. Inspirations come from the country, primitive peasant cultures, the Orient, Italy and almost any period of the past. Home furnishings trends are a reaction to the realities of our lives. What are our realities?

The 20–34 age group makes up about one fourth of the total U.S. population. The weight of these numbers is influencing the country's life-style.

This generation has reached maturity in streamlined anterooms, open-plan schools and far-out discotheques. It's a generation whose eyes have grown accustomed to contemporary styles, a generation that is more familiar with the names of Eames and Breuer than with Chippendale and Hepplewhite. As these younger people mature and gain buying power, the contemporary styles that they prefer will become more and more prominent and popular. Even now manufacturers selling contemporary are doing better business, and traditional manufacturers are introducing contemporary collections.

This postwar generation is not interested in formal social encounters. Their social style has brought in a new era of informality, honesty and sensuality. "Design is more comfort-oriented now," notes New York furniture designer John Mascheroni. "The same trend that influenced the popularity of blue jeans a few years ago has relaxed the entire American way of living."

The squishy, molded polyurethane comfort, the butter-soft leathers and the sensual shapes of Italian furniture have had great appeal on the American market. Realizing where the action is, American manufacturers have followed suit.

The younger people were determined to be individualistic and "do their own thing." What started as an act of defiance has become a national way of life. Today everybody is doing his own thing. In furnishing, it is socially acceptable, indeed desirable, to be individualistic.

Most of us move away from home.

The old feeling of community and the sense of "belonging" it can engender are gone. Very few of us stay where we were born. Children often can't afford to establish homes in the same community as their parents, or they are motivated by a sense of adventure (or escape) to explore other territory. Corporate decision-makers uproot and relocate families constantly.

Because people are more and more mobile and cannot spend unlimited amounts each time they move, they require furniture that is easily transported, that can be arranged and rearranged in different homes and that can be added to or subtracted from as the needs arise. Modular furniture, designed like pieces of a puzzle that can be arranged infinitely, offers the option of instant transplant.

[handwritten margin note: Modular furniture]

People want their favorite familiar things around them—old family furniture, treasures from travels, whatever brings back happy memories and makes them feel good. Today designers are more understanding of one's emotional need for these things. They've learned to work with them and incorporate them into "eclectic" interiors.

The divorce rate is above 50 percent.

The statisticians give credence to those that bemoan the disintegration of the family. Self-realization has superseded family welfare as the goal of our society. Writer Tom Wolfe calls the present population "The Me Generation." Single-person households are proliferating.

Today people expect the nest to provide the security and love not found elsewhere. Soft seating, thick rugs, warm fabrics and old treasures can be as comforting as hot soup on a cold day. Such creature comforts can soothe the soul, even in a strange place.

We are living in smaller, more indistinctive spaces.

Increasing numbers of people consider the large, sprawling residences of the 1960s to be unnecessary and wasteful of energy. While in 1960, 70 percent of the housing starts were single-family dwellings, the figure in 1976 plummeted to 40 percent. It is projected that by 1980 only 30 percent of the housing starts will be single-family units.

Anonymous stamped-out space prevails in today's high-rise housing. Even the rich are having to come to terms with the fact that a standardized concrete shell has become the bare bones of contemporary urban design.

As a result, home furnishings manufacturers and interior designers strive to create a sense of space. Traditional styles are reproduced in smaller scale, often with the details simplified. Functional furniture is made from materials that look lightweight so that it won't seem to take much space. Glass and see-through plastic, mirror and reflective metal, wicker and rattan are popular. Multipurpose furniture—such as sleep-sofas and wall storage systems—gives flexibility to a limited space. Furniture that folds or collapses is also useful. Much furniture is designed to take advantage of vertical space.

Designers respond to smaller spaces in either of two ways—through illusion or through minimalism.

They can create the illusion of a larger space by opening up the barriers between rooms, by playing tricks with mirrors or deep-perspective wallcoverings, by connecting the indoors with the outdoors.

The other answer is liberation through limitation. The designer strives to find the simplest possible solution to his client's needs; it may end in platforms or in piles of pillows. A simple, minimal background does not tell people how to behave in the space. It allows multipurpose flexibility. It also keeps the place airy and uncrowded—so it seems more spacious!

Interest in ecology and the energy crisis have brought us back to nature. Reawakened respect for nature has led us to recycling resources, to health food and even exercise.

Designers realized that the back-to-nature movement could provide an emotional source of strength. Nature prevails over the passage of time and the traumas of the day.

Designers popularized natural materials and earth-tone colors. While thinking "country," it was easy to romance the peasant peoples and their charming naïve designs. Designers turned to the handcrafts of simpler cultures—Turkish kilim rugs, Indonesian batiks, Mexican molas, American patchwork.

Nixon opened trade with China.

After his trip, we began to import baskets, brooms, what-have-you. Interior designers began to use a lot of basketry. They moved on to an occasional piece of rattan or wicker, which worked well with either traditional or contemporary styles. Manufacturers noticed what the designers were doing and started making more furniture of wicker, rattan and bamboo.

Thinking of Nixon's trip to China made some people recall the influence of the Orient in the past and revive traditional Oriental styles and accents.

We celebrated the nation's Bicentennial.

The Bicentennial awakened our awareness of our heritage—and our desire to preserve it. It prompted a rash of restoration work and encouraged many manufacturers to emphasize their historic restoration or reproduction capacities.

The Bicentennial made people think about their own personal heritage and history. "The universal appeal of *Roots*," explains author Alex Haley, "is based on the average American's longing for a sense of heritage."

The celebration engendered respect for the traditional furnishing styles that have endured the test of time. Traditional styles bespeak history and heritage. They provide a respectable refuge from the confusion of changing times—an emotional source of sustenance.

Pleasure in the past has taken many forms. Young consumers are nostalgic about times they never lived. They haunt antique shops and auctions. Others pick the period of the past that appeals to their personality—Art Deco for slick chic, Victorian for cute quaintness, 18th-century English for timeless elegance.

The "Treasures of Tutankhamun" Egyptian exhibit is on tour.

At its opening in Washington, the exhibit caused incomparable crowds and unmeasurable excitement. The impact of the exhibition can already be seen in the home furnishings field. New bed and bath linens, wallpapers, fabrics, accessories and art objects are on the market. The motifs of the lotus, the lion and hieroglyphics, the colors of ocher, carnelian and turquoise are already attracting attention.

More people are making more money than ever before.

We are a vast middle class. In what other country would a garbageman be making $20,000 a year? In spite of all the belly-aching and ballyhoo about the American economy, the U.S. has been on a business boom ever since the wartime spending of the 1940s. The boom has pumped money into every level of society on a scale unprecedented in any other country in the history of the world.

It's hard to find help these days. Most people have to take care of their own homes, and they don't want to spend their leisure time cleaning. They are demanding furnishings that are easy-care. Plastics were made for our maidless day. Durable, washable plastics show up in laminated surfaces such as Formica, in clear finishes for floors and tabletops such as polyurethane, in leather-look upholsteries and washable wallcoverings of vinyl, in sculpted furniture of rigid plastic. Fabrics today are usually either washable or treated with dirt-repellent finishes such as Scotchgard or Zepel.

People are spending more money on their homes. They want comfort, individuality and, often, relief from the sterility of the architecture. They are looking for quality, but most are confused and need help.

Department stores, furnishings specialty stores, and large chain stores are offering assistance. Increasingly, they are showing model rooms so the consumer can see the whole package pulled together. They are hiring design-trained professionals to sell furnishings, and many stores are opening design studios that offer an interior design service to their customers.

Many interior designers are joining stores that want to beef up their design departments. Others are taking private clients with modest to moderate budgets. Many big-name designers are designing reasonably priced products for the home. The sheet field is studded with stars. An upholstery collection, designed by New York designer Angelo Donghia, has just been introduced. Today there is more general awareness and demand for good design. Designers are delighted to respond.

How do home furnishings trends actually happen?

Some designer is sensitive to the temper of the times and imaginatively chooses materials that answer emotional needs as well as practical requirements. Someone in the news media discovers the idea and publishes it. Furniture designers see the newspapers and magazines. They see the new "look" and find it exciting. They begin using the concept in their work.

Leading manufacturers produce designs incorporating "the look" and show them to the retail store buyers at the wholesale furniture market in High Point, North Carolina. The store buyers purchase this merchandise and display it in their stores' model rooms.

Customers are turned on to the "look" by what they see in the magazines and in the model rooms. They begin to want what they see. Because of the customer demand for the "look," more and more manufacturers jump on the bandwagon, producing merchandise with the "look." As styles work down the ladder, so do prices (and usually quality).

Designers begin it all. They have the imagination to understand our needs—our practical needs *and* our psychic needs. They know the materials, styles and technologies available and select those that will not only solve our problems but also lighten our spirits and make us happy in our homes. Designers set the home furnishings trends of the times.

PART ONE
Survey of New Home Furnishings Products

What's New?

Keep your eye on what designers are doing. Products they like and use will ultimately become available on the retail market. For example, a few years ago when it first came out, the Parsons table was used only by designers. Now it's everywhere. Étagères also. Karl Springer, Ltd., an innovative manufacturer to the trade, was one of the first to laminate fabrics and leathers to tables and then give them exotic finishes. Now the idea is pretty common on the mass market. Designers started using wicker indoors. Now everybody's doing it. Designers specified very expensive suede sofas; now less-expensive versions are on the retail market. Wall systems and platform beds were ideas that appealed to designers. Now people are generally attracted. Once designers have accepted an idea, it's bound to get on the mass market in some version.

What you don't see in designer rooms will also tell you something—that the idea is already passé or was never really accepted in the first place. Swagged chain lamps are an example of an idea that was never accepted; arc lamps are an example of an idea that's outdated. The arc lamp was used so often and reproduced in so many versions that designers became tired of it and wanted to move on to something else. Designers have to clean out their inventory of ideas periodically in order to go on to new things—which leads us to the question of fashion.

Fashion is change. Change keeps us young, keeps us feeling fresh, keeps us from being bored. This is not to say that you shouldn't cherish your old arc lamp, your old comfy shoes or your old worn jeans. You should have what you like. Designers can find ways to make even your old favorite objects look fresh—sometimes simply by rearranging them.

Home furnishings is becoming a fashion field. The idea that furnishings should last the rest of our lives is losing force. People aren't afraid of buying a new car that lasts two years. A woman is not afraid to buy a $150 dress that she wears only on special occasions. Why should a sofa be asked to endure forever? People are beginning to realize that they *do* become bored with the same old furnishings, that they want the uplift of something new.

An old investment need not be discarded. Today's preference for an "eclectic" mixture of styles allows an imaginative mix of the old and the new. An old object can be integrated into a new mixture, or it may be retired to a closet and stored until it comes back into style or seems fresh again. (Think of the people who wish they had kept some of the objects they had in the 1930s. Wouldn't they have fun with them today?) Your environment is a living, growing thing—just as you are. It should change and adapt just like you do.

The Designer Market

What are the new products on the designer market? The pages following will show you some. Wicker and bamboo furniture are big—part of the natural look. For the ultimate in comfort the fat and squishy Italian look in upholstery is *it*. Luxurious fabrics such as printed suedes and satins are in vogue. And for a touch of the exotic, designers are selecting tables derived from animal forms and shapes. Tables might stand on legs shaped like elephant trunks or on feet that look like animal paws.

The designer market is like the tippy-top of a pyramid. It is here where innovative ideas begin, where the unheard-of is heard of. An idea might be born in a conference between an interior designer and a manufacturer when the designer asks for something special for a client. Later, after the product is installed, others may see it; the media might photograph it and the idea may make waves through the entire home furnishings industry. Designers dare to be different; it's part of their stock-in-trade. Designer sources accommodate those differences. Many manufacture exclusively to custom order. These manufacturers require knowledgeable clients who understand what they are ordering and how it will look when installed. Other designer sources deal in such expensive or in such unusual objects that their market is necessarily limited—limited to those who know a good investment from a bad one and a tiresome trinket from a treasure. A designer's knowledge can protect the consumer from disaster.

Some manufacturers have their own research and development departments and their own inspired product designers. These companies generate innovative ideas that attract designers. One would think that they would attract the general public also, but to date it has not been so. Knoll, a company that has manufactured many a modern masterpiece—Saarinen's pedestal table, Mies van der Rohe's Barcelona chair, just to name two—hasn't made it on the retail level, although the company has tried twice. Both the venture at Georg Jensen in 1969 and at Bloomingdale's in 1974 failed. Perhaps the prices were too high. Perhaps no one wanted to pay for the perfect quality of original designs when less-expensive copies were plentiful. Too bad. Original designs, like antiques, grow in value. Meanwhile, one has the pleasure of perfection.

Many people question the exclusivity of the designer market, the showrooms "to the trade only." Why won't these showrooms sell to a retail customer? Often the answer is because the designer's understanding and expertise protects them from your displeasure. They are not set up to serve the public. They don't have the space to accommodate a lot of people. They don't have the staff to answer a lot of questions. They don't have the stock to deliver; many manufacture in limited quantities or just to custom-order. The designers are the ones who appreciate them and do business with them, and they would rather just keep on doing business with them rather than risk the designers' ire by doing business with you.

Many designer showrooms will welcome you if accompanied by your designer. It's like taking a trip, and the designer is the tour guide, telling you about the things you see and relating things to your own interests. Your designer can keep you steering on course through the myriad merchandise in the showrooms and keep you from losing your sense of identity and your dollars and cents!

Fabric houses often don't allow designers to bring in their clients. It's better to have the designer select samples of four or five fabrics that would work for you and have you pick the one you would prefer in the sane surroundings of your own home. Looking at a lot of fabrics can drive most normal people crazy with confusion.

Designer sources are all over the country. In Part Three of this book there is a Directory of Designer Sources and Showrooms. Showrooms are listed in Atlanta, Boston, Chicago, Dallas, Los Angeles, Miami, New York, Philadelphia and San Francisco. Unfortunately, we lacked the space to list those in Cleveland, Denver, Milwaukee, Seattle and all the other many cities that offer sources to the trade. But your designer knows where to find what you want. It's his business.

In most major cities designer showrooms are clustered in a certain area of town or even in a certain group of buildings. This proximity of showrooms makes it easier for you and your designer to shop comfortably and conveniently.

The showroom may be a manufacturer's showroom or a representative's showroom. Manufacturers set up their own showroom in an area when their volume of business warrants it. Otherwise, they have representatives. Manufacturers' reps are often marvelously inventive people who assemble their own assortment of manufacturers to represent. They make the melange to create their own "look." Often people running representative showrooms travel the world, sleuthing around for exciting ideas and unusual objects that will turn on their designer-clients. These people generate a lot of excitement in the industry, and they tailor their lines for the specific tastes of people in their area.

If a market isn't active enough to warrant a representative showroom, then there's bound to be a traveling salesman or at least a mailman who will deliver manufacturers' catalogs to a designer.

There's a wondrous wealth of fine furnishings out there to be uncovered with the help of a designer. You can hire an independent designer or use one from the design department of a retail store.

The Retail Market
Truth to tell, the retail market ain't what it used to be. It's much better! People are more affluent and educated these days. They have more discretionary income to spend on home furnishings—*and* more discretion. They are demanding quality, and increasingly they are demanding fashion flair. In addition to copying designer lines, mass manufacturers are developing some of their own originals.

Consider what has happened to clothing. Designers of couturier clothes have been designing ready-to-wear and putting their names or initials on everything. People are falling all over themselves buying these "name" brands. Names sell.

People in home furnishings have seen the writing on the wall (or on the shirts and scarves) and are trying to grab some of the glamor. Sheet manufacturers have invited practically every name designer to make up a bed. Most of the names they've invited have been from the clothing fashion field. Some of these creative talents have moved from clothing to sheets and on to other home furnishings. Halston is doing rugs. Gloria Vanderbilt is doing dishes.

Naturally enough, those people who have made a profession of product design in the home furnishings field feel frustrated. Their names aren't known to the public. Their names are not buying buzz words, but still they are the ones who know the technology of machines, who know how to master them to make fine furnishings. John Mascheroni, a leading New York furniture designer, explains the problem: "Manufacturers have traditionally viewed the product designer as a tool, a creative means to an end. They've overlooked the fact that a designer can also sell and promote merchandise." Times are a-changing.

The mass-manufacturer Kroehler recently introduced a moderately priced upholstery line created by Angelo Donghia, an outstanding interior designer who has long been making custom designs for his clients. "High style and high prices need not be irrevocably linked," notes Donghia. "I want to create luxury that is affordable for real, everyday living."

Large portions of the public know the names of the modern masters of furniture design—Marcel Breuer, Mies van der Rohe, Eero Saarinen, Charles Eames, to name a few. Usually the best people can do is to buy fairly good copies of the authentic original designs. They look for them by name.

Knoll is the manufacturer of many of the modern masters. "Quite frankly," admits company president Bobby Cadwallader, "we are tired of making the 'pilot chair' everybody else knocks off. Knoll believes it can compete with the mass-production furniture makers at their price with originality. We will still be doing prestige work. Now we will also have chairs so good that professionals will be proud to specify them at low prices." And most likely their designers will be known by name.

Designer "names" are not only a means of sales promotion. Product designers are living, breathing people who try to understand what people need and want so that they can engineer the answers. Milo Baughman, the outstanding designer behind the success of Thayer Coggin contemporary furniture, recently explained to an audience of design-school seniors that communicating with the consumer was the secret of success. (Think of clothing again and Diane von Furstenberg. She, more than Freud, understood what a woman wanted.) Home furnishings manufacturers today are beginning to realize that a good designer is worth his weight in gold. Because of this, distinctions between designer lines and retail lines are fuzzing. More and more quality furniture is appearing on the mass market.

Wallcoverings and Fabrics

Next to paint, wallcoverings and/or fabrics are the most inexpensive way to change the look of your home. They can freshen the face of a home that's grown tired. They can make an empty room feel furnished. A dull or dreary room gains instant personality and pizzazz with a patterned wallcovering. A small room can seem stretched if walls and large furniture are in a matching subtle pattern. Diverse and dissimilar upholstered pieces can work up a harmonious family feeling if covered in the same fabric. A patterned wallcovering or fabric can inspire or pull together a color scheme. Designers use fabrics and wallcoverings to solve problems.

Because the wallcoverings and fabrics used in a room (or in adjacent rooms) should coordinate compatibly, many manufacturers are in the business of making coordinated collections. Fabrics often have matching wallcoverings, and, if not, the fabric itself may be put on the wall.

What does a designer have to decide when selecting a wallcovering or fabric? First he has to choose a material that will do the job required, that will stand up to the wear it will get while providing aesthetic assets.

In choosing a wallcovering, a designer might select vinyl because it is washable or fabric because it insulates and absorbs sound. He might choose foil because it reflects light or a texture because it gives a sense of dimension through the play of light and shadow.

In choosing a fabric he must consider where and how it will be used. Will it be used at the window to filter light and provide privacy? If so, it might be a light open-weave casement. Will it be used for slipcovers and drapery? If so, a medium-weight fabric would be fine. Will it be upholstery? Anything from a medium- to a heavyweight will work. Closely woven unshiny matte-finished fabrics can stand heavy wear. A shiny glazed finish can rub right off the seat of a much-used chair, but otherwise it's easy maintenance. Dirt will shake right off it.

The fibers of the material must have the right look and performance characteristics, plus price. The fabric may be washable, no-iron, fire-retardant, dirt-repellent, moth-resistant, fade-resistant—whatever necessary. Designers generally prefer fabrics made from the natural fibers—cotton, wool, linen, silk. Price and performance characteristics of synthetics often make blends of natural and synthetic fibers desirable. Those on a budget can find synthetic materials that simulate the natural look. Specialty fabrics such as casements are most often made from synthetic fibers.

The width of the fabric is a particular concern for slipcovers and upholstery. A designer doesn't want a seam showing up at the wrong place. If the pattern allows, a designer might turn the fabric and use it along its length instead of its width. This process, called "railroading," saves seaming.

Colors are a concern. Should the effect be sharp and dramatic, or soft and subtle? Cool, warm, or neutral? A pattern is usually available in a variety of color combinations. These are called "colorways." "Stock" colorways are those that the manufacturer has in stock on his shelves. "Custom" colors are made to order and usually require a minimum yardage.

Patterns can be inspired by anything in the world. Nature and geometry have been inspirations always. Almost every culture in history has interpreted these themes in its own manner. The scale or size may be large or small. The design may be drawn boldly or delicately. The colors convey the preferences of the time. Oriental and simple/country or exotic/ethnic interpretations seem to have permanent popularity.

Traditional designs are often copied from an original antique pattern, called a "document." The copy is called "a documentary design." An "authentic documentary design" copies the original faithfully. Many traditional patterns are restyled and recolored in today's preferred palette. Blending the old and the new, these designs work right in to today's "eclectic" interiors.

The pattern "repeat" tells the size of the pattern. If a pattern repeats itself every two inches, the design is small-scale. If it takes 27 inches before a pattern repeats, it is large-scale. Generally, designs should be in proportion to the size of the area where they are used. However, dramatic large-scale designs in bright colors can be used in rooms where you don't spend a great deal of time. Small-scale designs are good mixers and can go almost anywhere. On the wall they give a textured appearance.

Manufacturers use many methods to coordinate fabrics and wallcoverings:

(Top right) ALBERT VAN LUIT's "Sweet William" is a large-scale (27″ repeat) motif of bouquets on a silhouetted lattice. The vinyl wallcovering matches the cotton/rayon fabric.

(Bottom right) REED's "Trees" and "Colgate" patterns are printed both as wallcoverings and fabrics. They are the same colors.

The Material Must Suit Its Purpose

Many patterns are printed on a variety of grounds—on cloths in weights from heavy to sheer, with finishes from matte to glazed and on wallcoverings from plastic to paper, from shiny to textured. Woven patterns and textures tend toward airy, open casements or dense and durable upholstery weaves.

Casement Fabrics

1. PROUTY DESIGNS offers a lightweight, open-weave casement called "Furrow." The durable net design is woven of flameproof Verel, versatile drapable rayon, and a touch of flax for a natural look. The fabric width is 50". Casement fabrics are usually seamed to be double the width of the window.

7. CORAL OF CHICAGO prints "Printemps" on crisp acetate or on a blend of fire-retardant modacrylic and washable polyester.

11. DECORATORS WALK shows a sheer casement with a woven design that offers interest as well as light filtering. Woven of Belgian linen, cotton and a little rayon, the casement has a natural look.

Multi-purpose Fabrics

2. STROHEIM & ROMANN has printed durable sailcloth in three compatible small-scale patterns, "Paradox," "Paralex" and "Pyramid."

3. SHAWN TABIN's "Rosetti" is a multipurpose printed cotton imported from Heal, Britain's famous fabric source. This design

of small motifs has a large-scale coordinate for variety and verve.

4. DAVID AND DASH shows "Nocture," a versatile 54"-wide cotton. A coordinating pattern picks up the small-check detail of the background.

5. BORIS KROLL prints the large-repeat design "Sea Grapes," on two qualities of cotton to make it appropriate for a variety of applications.

12. SCHUMACHER knows that stripes are beautiful blenders. In this particular collection 65 colors are stocked. The 54"-wide materials are versatile viscose rayon.

Mostly Upholstery

6. BORIS KROLL's "Madagascar" is a jacquard woven rayon/cotton upholstery fabric, but some people have put it on panels because it is so graphic.

8. ETALAGE picked fresh vegetables as quilted design motifs. Here is "Ratatouille." All patterns can be quilted on a large choice of fabrics, such as chintzes, wools, satins, backed by a soft Dacron batting and gauze.

9. KIRK-BRUMMEL offers "Barbary," a flamestitch design that defies time. For upholstery, the design is embroidered on soft Belgian linen velvet. For wallcovering, the design may be custom-printed on vinyl, paper or jute.

10. SCALAMANDRÉ, known for its fine selection of formal fabrics, imports "Guardi" from Belgium. A lampas weave, the fabric is as beautiful from one side as the other. It may be used for drapery as well as for upholstery.

7

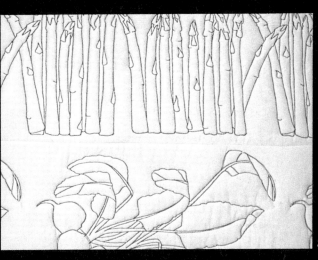
8

9

10

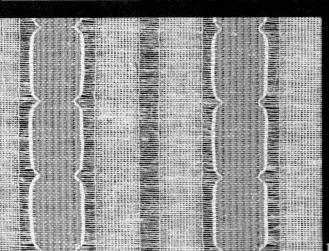
11

12

Designs/Colors
May Be Historic or Modern

1

2

3

Sometimes the distinction between traditional and contemporary is none too clear. The past is the prologue to the present, and so its themes and dreams infuse our consciousness.

The glitter and glamour of the 1930s and its Art Deco designs seem to satisfy today's slick sophisticate. Fashion couturier Valentino of Rome has designed a line of home furnishings fabrics that has caused happy hoopla in the trade. The designs are largely inspired by the 1930s, with large and small-scaled nature motifs often appearing on sultry dark fields. Dark Deco colors like navy and rich reddish brown are part of today's trends.

Those yearning for romance and relief from slick sophistication can find it in Victoriana. Welsh designer Laura Ashley has made news and set trends with her small-scale, musty-dusty colored Victorian designs. Now Victorian roses can be seen almost anywhere, and "dusty" colors are a definite fashion trend.

What could be older or more historic than ancient Egypt? The Egyptian exhibits traveling the country are causing contemporary home furnishing fashions to adopt the motifs and colors of the Nile. Terra-cotta, slate, turquoise, black and gold are in vogue.

Our improved relations with China have opened our eyes to the timeless attributes of Oriental art. Bright, bold lacquer colors give sharp, pleasing, teasing accents to contemporary interiors.

And can you call natural colors contemporary or traditional? Is a tree timely? Natural earth-tone colors are fashion favorites.

Traditional designs are a living legacy that are a constant inspiration to the present. Designers pick from the past those styles and colors that meaningfully meet the mood of the day.

The most truly traditional designs are those that are actual, literal copies of those from the past. These are called "documentary" designs or, more precisely, "authentic historic reproductions."

With the coming of the nation's Bicentennial the country was caught in "Restoration Fever." Local historical societies moved into action, trying to freshen and refurbish the homes of their towns' founding fathers. They asked the assistance of many manufacturers, who painstakingly recreated and restored the original designs. After the completion of the restorations, many manufacturers made their collections of "documentary" designs available to interior designers for use in homes that might not be so old. Designs are often offered in the original "documentary" colorway, plus others.

Traditional

(Left) REED LTD., a Canada-based wallcovering manufacturer, was asked to help in the restoration of 14 historic homes built between 1707 and 1880 from Virginia to Rhode Island. The original wallpapers were studied by Charles S. Freedman, ASID, and then carefully recreated. The collection of 30 exquisite documentary designs is now offered to the trade.

1. Original festoon pattern wallpaper
2. Reproduction in the Glanmore House, Belleville, Ontario
4. Original wallpaper imported from Europe circa 1734
3. The reproduction as it looks today in the Hancock-Clarke House, Lexington, Massachusetts

Contemporary

(Right) Contemporary designs have moved from bold colors, hard-edged supergraphics and flat-faced flowers into an emphasis on texture and natural earth colors.

REED LTD's "Percussion," the intricate stripe design here, has the look of a woven texture. The stripe adapts equally well to a ceiling-stretching vertical application, a calming horizontal application or a dynamic diagonal application. It is part of the Bolta Tex brand wallcovering collection, manufactured by General Tire & Rubber.

Mixing Patterns

1, 2, 3. FRANCISCAN FABRICS makes a mix of "Marley," a little leaf design, "Marley Plaid," the same little leaves with a large overprinted trellis design and "Summer," a simple scaled-down trellis design. All are printed on Belgian linen.

4. ANDRE MATENCIOT coordinates "Eleanore," a richly detailed floral with "Stars Above," a sparse small-scaled geometric. The geometric picks one color from the flowers and mixes it with white. The designs are printed on fabrics and wallpapers.

5, 8. SCHUMACHER offers a coordinated collection of fabrics and wallpapers designed by Vera. Similarity of colors and boldness or delicacy of design make for compatible companions.

6. WALL TRENDS INTERNATIONAL has a collection of coordinating small-scale vinyl-coated wallpapers. Pictured are "Bessie," a floral pattern with a 7″ repeat, and "Joan," a diamond pattern that picks up the pink in a 2″ repeat. Both designs mix with other small patterns, as well as with basket-weave textured solids.

7. STROHEIM & ROMANN combines similarly elegant, delicate designs—a printed floral "Shingu" and a striped lisere "Lindezza."

9. ABRAHAM-ZUMSTEG imports Swiss fabrics from a firm that has been supplying leading European couturiers. Each design and each color group is comprised of positive and negative prints, small details picked out of large patterns, and juxtapositions of colors and motifs. The mixing and matching possibilities are endless. Here, "Westminster" and two variations of "Fleur de Fleur."

1

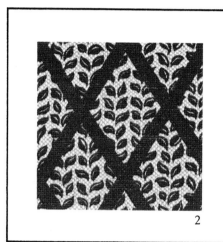

2

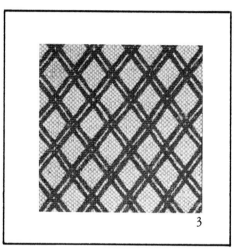

3

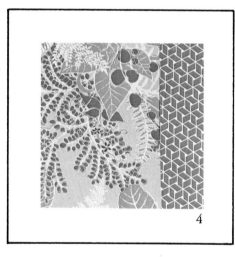

4

5

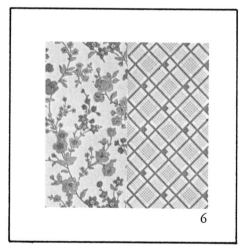

6

7

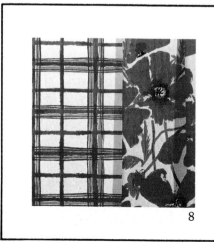

8

9

Country vs. City

10. WAVERLY offers the *Village Crafts Collection* of 18th-century document-inspired patterns. Each pattern is reproduced in the original colorway, plus others. Here, "Fiske Stencil," a bird and flower print on fabric and wallpaper.

11, 13. S.M. HEXTER imports a collection of clean, straight-lined, reversible woven patterns from the renowned Kinnasand textile manufacturer in Sweden. "Karl Oskar" is the stripe. "Lycka" is the patchwork.

12. BRUNSCHWIG & FILS shows a charming naïve pattern of a bird with strawberries set in an overall lattice pattern. Two cameo images are perfectly spaced for upholstering chair seats and backs.

14. BRUNSCHWIG & FILS' "Gaspard," a canvas cloth, is a sturdy water-repellent cotton, in red, yellow, green and blue.

15. S. M. HEXTER has a collection of three large-repeat patchworks that correlate with 15 small-scale geometric and floral motifs. "Le Patchwork Jardin" pictured has a 56½" repeat.

16. ALBERT VAN LUIT's *Sequel Collection*, designed by John Leigh Spath, is suitable for the sophisticate. "Crown Imperial" is an Art Nouveau-style blossom printed on a shiny foil wallcovering and on an ethereal sheer.

17. JACK LENOR LARSEN makes magic—a sparkling city sensation—with "Houdini," a reversible woven. Part of the spell is bound with metallic threads.

18. ODENHEIMER & BAKER's "Homage to Vuillard" is a tribute to Jean Edouard Vuillard, a turn-of-the-century artist.

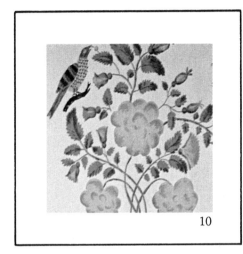

10

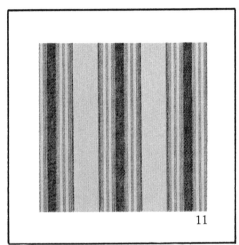

11

12

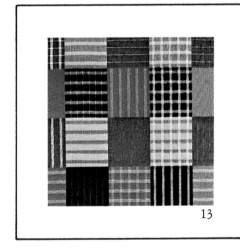

13

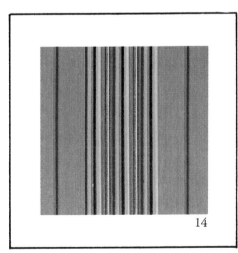

14

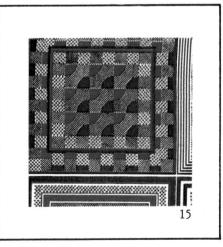

15

16

17

18

Nature—The Constant Inspiration

1. BRUNSCHWIG & FILS presents "La Rose." The pretty painterly rendition of blossoms and buds is soft and romantic, while the fabric itself is a practical and useful 59"-wide cotton. SCHUMACHER offers a collection of French fabrics and wallcoverings made exclusively for it by the Paris firm Pierre Frey. All fabric designs are printed on 54"-wide cotton, in glazed or matte finishes. Nature's inspiration takes many forms.

2. "Les Tuileries" is inspired by a documentary design.

3. "Chateau Loire," printed in impressively delicate detail, is traditional in treatment, complete with bird on branch.

14. "Perigot," with its simplified, abstracted tiny floral branches, has a contemporary feeling.

15. "Forest Sauvage" recalls the pleasing, primitive style of the French painter Henri Rousseau.

SCHUMACHER regularly asks a selection of leading interior designers from across the country to examine its library of documentary designs, to choose an old pattern that pleases and then to reinterpret it in a multiuse fabric for today's times.

4. "Nostell," a glazed cotton, was inspired by a wallpaper and companion chintz found in Nostell Priory—an 18th-century English country house. It was adapted by William D. Bowden, ASID, co-owner of the venerable Seattle firm, William L. Davis Co.

6. "Parish Magnolia," a glazed cotton, is a floral design found on a

1

2

3

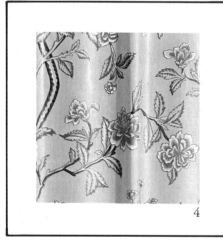

4

5

6

7

8

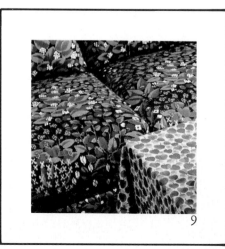

9

19th-century drapery panel interpreted by Mrs. Henry Parish II, head of Parish-Hadley, the prestigious New York design firm.

13. "Colorado," a cotton print taken from an early 20th-century fabric, has been enlivened by H. Albert Phibbs, ASID, president of his own firm in Denver.

5, 9. ABRAHAM-ZUMSTEG is a firm formed to import the special Swiss fabrics designed by Gustav Zumsteg and Frederico Forquet (Italian couturier turned interior designer). The designers looked to nature and found fish ("Sea Jewels") and wonderful wild flowers ("Mille Fleur" and "Buttercup").

7, 8. STROHEIM & ROMANN picks flowers inspired by the rich, heavy fabrics used in European country estates of the 17th and 18th centuries. Called *La Collection des Grands Musées,* the group includes tapestries, cut velvets, brocades and liseres.

10. BRUNSCHWIG & FILS' "Grandiflora" is a detailed botanical study printed with 28 screens on white cotton.

11. BOB MITCHELL hand-screen prints patterns on paper to achieve the subtle textural effects that give a sense of dimension to flat walls. "Jana" is part of the *Designs West Four* wallcovering collection.

12, 17. KIRK-BRUMMEL celebrated spring with cherry blossoms ("Laura") and iris ("Jennifer"). The floral profusion is the work of award-winning Welsh designer Laura Ashley.

16. EAGLESHAM's "Geraniums" are planted on cotton in seven stock colorways, or custom colors.

18. DESIGNFRIENDS, LTD. plays a "Shell Game" on the walls. The pattern is shown printed on Kraft paper (which looks like grocery bags).

Timeless Influence of the Orient

1. SCHUMACHER's "Kama Kura" design of formalized holly-hocks with peony hearts is inspired by an old Japanese obi sash and interpreted by designer John B. Wisner. It is printed on a 54"-wide cotton.

2. VALENTINO PIU's trend-setting and stylish collections also find inspiration in the Orient. "Chinese Waves" in bright, bold colors coordinates with a similarly colored stripe. Both are 52" cottons.

3. S. M. HEXTER allows dragons to consort with butterflies in "Ho Chang," a handsome cotton print available in six colorways, including cucumber and curry, black and spice brown.

4. BORIS KROLL has a collection called *Shibui*, which in Japanese means "elegant." The fabrics are exquisitely detailed and colored in lusciously luxurious soft shell colors. Every color and pattern has several coordinates. Did pattern-on-pattern begin in the Orient?

5. LEE/JOFA sees serenity in the Oriental view of nature. "Oriental Water Flowers" includes beautifully drawn birds among the lilies. The cotton fabric's flowered borders provide an interesting panel effect.

6. JACK LENOR LARSEN not only sees serenity; he sees "Shangri-La"! His paradise is hidden in the clouds, in hills drawn with the ambiguous perspectives characteristic of Oriental art.

1

2

3

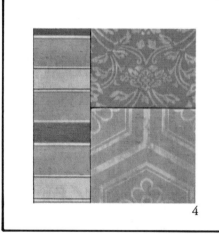

4

5

6

7

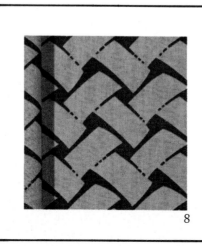

8

9

The dream scene is printed on a 50" cotton/linen cloth.

7. GREEFF has a collection called *Mandarin Tree.* Styled by Virginia Nepodal, the collection uses traditional Oriental motifs such as the lotus, peacocks, tea chests and, here, "Coromandel Screen." (Putting this printed pattern on folding panels could create the same effect as an actual Coromandel screen—a lot cheaper!)

8. SCHUMACHER found the traditional tatami mat to be the inspiration for "La Toscane," a woven texture pattern, in its French *Pierre Frey* collection of cottons and companion wallcoverings.

9. SCHUMACHER offers a collection of fabrics inspired by Wedgwood china. The original Wedgwood—Josiah—was an 18th-century Englishman who, like others of his era, was influenced by trade with the East. "Ming Jade" pictured here is one of nine patterns in the Schumacher collection, printed on a 54" linen/cotton blend. A matching wallcovering is available.

10. ALBERT VAN LUIT's director of design, John Leigh Spath, was moved by the serene sight of a single tree to recreate the scene in a wallcovering. "Miyako" is printed on two 27"-wide panels of shimmering textured foil and hung along with plain panels. Van Luit has been producing sectional scenic wallcoverings since its founding in the 1930s.

10

The Appeal of the Exotic

Those faraway places with the strange-sounding names have always been calling. Imagine Columbus, Gauguin, the Spanish conquistadors. During the reigns of King Henry VIII and Queen Elizabeth, English ships explored the world and brought back Chinese pottery, porcelains, paintings, Turkish rugs, East Indian printed cottons.

The cultivated classes of 18th-century England and France collected refined objects from the Orient. So did our own sea captains. Exotic objects have long been symbols of wealth and worldly sophistication.

Something else is happening in our era—in our mechanized materialistic mass social system. Handcrafts no longer seem like loving-hands-at-home second-best; they are rare and unusual objects. Who today has the time—or skill? Some do indulge to prove they have leisure time; some are committed to their art, but most of the others of us buy imported handcrafts as a pleasing contrast to our mass-produced furnishings and also as a symbol of something simpler—some place, some culture somewhere in the world where life is uncomplicated and back with the basics.

A native craft that is particularly popular now is batik. True batiks are made from hand-pouring wax in patterns on fabric and then dyeing it. The dye does not penetrate the areas that are waxed. Designs and colors are built up by steps of waxing and dyeing. At the end all wax is removed by a solvent. Batik usually has a speckled or mottled quality. Today some manufacturers are able to create fabrics with a batiklike look through the more mechanized process of screen printing.

1. S. M. HEXTER features an extensive selection of batiks. Named the *East Wind Collection,* favorite and innovative batik patterns appear on 90 wallcoverings and 45 coordinating fabrics. The illustrated vignette depicts three of these.

2. CHINA SEAS offers an abundance of intricate Indonesian batiks. In addition, it hand-screen prints "Watteau," an intricate batik floral on a 45″ cotton fabric and on a matte vinyl wallcovering. A blue/yellow/white version is available on a heavy cotton.

3. ALBERT VAN LUIT's "Kapala" has a batiklike texture. The design was inspired by a detail from an Oriental fan and is part of the company's *Sequel Collection* of large-scale designs. The pattern is printed on a vinyl wallcovering and on fabrics of three weights— a heavy cotton blend, a middle-weight linen/rayon blend and a goat's-hair sheer.

4. I. D. INTERNATIONAL's offerings show the influence of the East. In addition to crewel embroideries from Kashmir, silks from Thailand and Korea, the company collects batiks from Indonesia. The batiks, or "wax writing" as the Javanese call them, come in brilliant blues, purples, magentas, greens and oranges. One of 80 fresh designs is pictured.

5. S. M. HEXTER is importing "Ikats." These exotic motifs, originally found in Malaysia, are characterized by blurred edges, similar to reflections in the water. Hexter found four of them in Guatemala plus a pleasing handwoven cotton stripe.

6. BRUNSCHWIG & FILS is copying kilims, the famous flat hand-woven rugs of Turkey, and printing the patterns on cloths of linen and cotton.

7. SCHUMACHER's *Designer's Choice* collection resurrects a documentary design depicting the legendary phoenix as it rises from its ashes. The delicately detailed batik document was reinterpreted by designer Jack Madison Rees, ASID, founder of Jack Rees Interiors, Kansas City, and editor of *Decorating with Color*.

8. GREEFF knows the appeal of the handmade, so it prints "Marabella" to look like an intricate embroidery stitch.

9. SCHUMACHER simulates petit-point handwork in its printed pattern, "Peaceable Kingdom." Elisabeth A. Lane, ASID, director of design at O'Neill and Bishop, chose to adapt the original documentary design.

10. LEE/JOFA offers actual "Crewel Embroidery," a stylish/timeless floral design stitched in wool on a cloth of natural cotton. Crewel embroideries inspired by the tree-of-life designs of India have had exotic appeal since the time of Henry VIII.

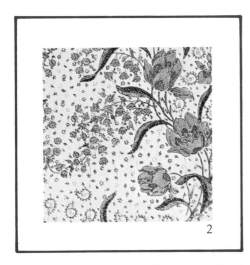

2

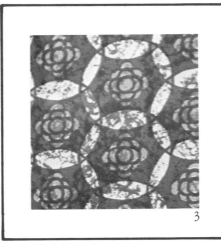

3

4

5

6

7

8

9

10

The Beautiful Bath

People have stopped thinking of the bathroom in simply utilitarian terms. What not long ago might have been considered the embarrassing requirements of personal hygiene are now considered inspirations for voluptuous sensual pleasures. With our new attitudes toward our bodies, the bathroom has become a sybaritic site.

More effort is being made today to make the bathroom a pretty place, a place for relaxation and refreshment. We, too, can celebrate our senses.

SHERLE WAGNER is a company that has long believed in beautifying the bath. Wealthy Italian film stars, Middle Eastern oil sheiks and internationally renowned jet-setters have found it a source of opulent appointments.

(Left) White marble and rose quartz were chosen for a Palm Beach bath.

(Right) A collection of hand-painted ceramic tiles (8″ x 8″) is offered in seven designs that coordinate with the Sherle Wagner Museum Collection of china basins and accessories. Each design adapts to individual interpretations. To make murals, blank tiles are mixed with the designs. The skill and craftsmanship shown in this tile work is rare indeed.

Rugs: Oriental and Contemporary

1

2

3

Rugs satisfy many of our needs today. Rugs have permanence because they're portable. You can roll up a rug not only for dancing but for moving. Rugs provide physical comfort. Not only do they insulate you from your neighbors' noise, but also they provide warmth to your toes. Multicolored patterned rugs are easy to maintain. Dirt and spills don't show. Such concealment is useful at entries, on staircases, in dining rooms—even in the kitchen.

Rugs furnish psychic satisfactions. An old Oriental provides a sense of heritage, even if you just bought it. An old family favorite rug conveys continuity and psychic security. A handmade rug, particularly from some romantic, faraway place, suggests refreshing reverie and an escape from the pressures of the day and its mass-produced sameness.

Interesting rugs can direct the decoration of a room. With a beautiful rug on the floor (or wall), you need not spend much money elsewhere. The colors of the rug will inspire the color scheme, and the pattern will usually provide all the patterned interest you need in the room. A small or medium-sized room should have a room-sized rug on the floor in order to avoid making the space seem cluttered. A large room may have several rugs, defining areas of activity. In any room—especially a cold or noisy one—a wall-hung rug makes a fine focal point.

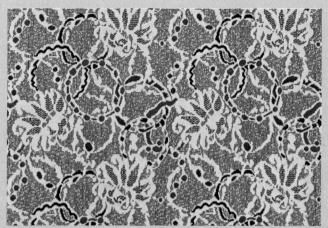

4

The world enjoys a heritage of ravishing rugs. Antiques exist and are a fabulous investment. Antiques are copied by hand and by machine. New designs are created constantly.

1. STARK offers a Bokhara pattern of the *Turkoman* type. Turkoman-type rugs were made by wild tribes who dyed their wools in the colors of blood and wove patterns in elementary geometric shapes.

2. GHIORDIAN KNOT shows an exquisite mid-19th-century Chinese pictorial rug. *Chinese* rugs are distinguished by backgrounds that make the principal color statement and by soft silk-like colors such as this salmon red.

3. SAXONY recreates the glory of Indian palaces in a new collection of dhurrie rugs, woven in cotton or wool. Floral and geometric patterns are stocked in soft and lovely grays and peaches, earth and sky tones. Custom colors are available.

4. PATTERSON, FLYNN & MARTIN offers Alan Campbell-designed rugs to go with Alan Campbell-designed fabrics and wall-coverings. Known for his fabrics, Campbell adapted his designs to create coordinates for the floor. The copyrighted carpets are 27" Wilton weaves. Shown is "Delilah," a bold interpretation of a small-scale 19th-century French damask pattern.

5. STARK is gathering a growing collection of exquisite flat-woven floor coverings. This reversible, all-wool double-weave is made in Rumania. Camels and ponies, doves and dinosaurs, fishes and turtles cavort and consort on both sides.

6. ROSECORE CARPET CO. has a collection of flat-woven wool dhurrie rugs stocked in two colorways and a variety of sizes: 6 x 9, 8 x 10, 8 x 12, 9 x 12 and 10 x 14. "Chin-Tu," pictured, is a striking geometric pattern.

5

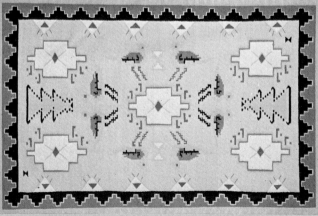

6

Oriental Rugs

Why buy an Oriental? The reasons are many. First, they are beautiful. They give warmth and richness to any decor—contemporary or traditional. Second, they are a safe investment. They have endured the test of time and won't go out of style. Antique Orientals are a better investment than most growth stocks you can name, and new ones are a good value for the money. Third, they are serviceable, durable designs. They wear and wear and wear.

What do you and your designer need to know about buying an Oriental? First of all, you need to establish your priorities. Do you want to purchase one primarily for the investment value? If so, you should work through a reputable dealer and buy an important antique. You can't care too much about the rug's size or colors, because with antiques you have to take what there is. Would you

rather have an Oriental of the right size and in the colors you prefer? If you have both luck and money, you might find an antique of the right specifications, but it is more likely that you will find what you want in a new rug.

Many old Oriental patterns are being reproduced today by hand and by machine. Machine-mades have existed since 1928, when the Marshall Field Company first introduced Oriental-pattern rugs made on high-speed tufting machines. Couristan and Karastan have become the leading suppliers of machine-tufted, wool-pile, Oriental-pattern rugs. Many styles are stocked in the stores. Some designer sources specialize in making such rugs to your custom colors and size. New Oriental rugs do not accrue value like the antiques, but if your new Oriental happens to be handmade, your grandchildren will probably be standing on something of value. Handwork is going by the boards as those Middle Eastern weavers leave their looms and join the new indus-

1

2

trial assembly lines where the benefits are better.

There are six main classifications of Oriental rugs. The Turkoman, Chinese, Persian, Caucasian and Turkish styles are shown. Indian rugs are characterized by flowers, leaves, vines and animals woven in a realistic manner, but today much of the Indian rug-weaving industry is devoted to reproducing precious Persian styles. The actual rugs are named after the areas where they were woven.

Chinese. The original manufacturers of silk, the Chinese applied silk dyes to their rugs.

1. SAXONY offers a Chinese silk Khotan rug.

Persian rugs are profusely decorated with the background barely showing. The patterns incorporate conventionalized flowers, animals, birds. The colors are soft, delicate and harmonious.

2. TREGANOWAN touts a Tabriz from the Summer Palace of the Russian czars.

3. AVAKIAN BROS. has a captivating Isfahan hunting rug.

4. NAHIGIAN BROS. shows the strong design of an 18th-century Bakhtiari Garden rug. The Bakhtiari are a powerful nomadic tribe ranging between Isfahan and Kermanshah in Persia.

5. HARMONY harbors a Shah Abbas hunting rug.

7. KENT-COSTIKYAN has a 19th-century Sarouk, a fine pile rug in dark reds and blues mixed with lighter colors.

Caucasian rugs are a product of a wild section of central Asia. They differ from Turkoman rugs in that they have more than blood colors, and the designs are more crowded and intricate.

6. PATTERSON, FLYNN & MARTIN displays a detail of a Caucasian dragon pattern.

Turkish rugs have patterns with ruler-sharp edges and colors that are bright, sharp and contrasting. The flat-woven kilims, initially woven by the peasant peoples for their own use, are particularly popular today.

8. BOCCIA, a specialist in kilims, exhibits a detail of a Yaruk.

RUGS: ORIENTAL AND CONTEMPORARY   31

Contemporary Rugs

There are still artists in the carpet craft. Some processes remain the same. Wool, the favored fiber, is said to be best when it is sheared from healthy sheep with long, resilient hair. "Dead wool," taken after the animal is killed, is reported to be brittle, to break and wear quickly. The wools must be washed with a mild detergent. Harsh detergents kill the life and luster of the wool. Dyes used must be the best.

The traditional techniques for making rugs are to weave them on a loom or to hand-tie knots into a structural grid. Today we have the technique of hand-tufting. Yarns are punched through the back of a specially constructed cotton cloth. The hand-tufting technique allows freedom from the traditional grid structure imposed by the loom. Anything is possible. The free-form shapes characteristic of much modern art can find expression in tufted textures for the floor (or walls).

V'Soske and Edward Fields are two companies that are in the avant-garde of carpet art. Their modern, custom-created patterns are achieved not only through variations of color but also through variations of texture and pile height. A great variety of yarns— from fine threads to bulky big ones—and techniques for carving or embossing the surface allow an infinity of textures.

These designer sources understand, and help create, the design trends of the times. Today's desire to get back to the basics shows

itself in natural textures, nature's colors and even nature-inspired subject matter.

(Left) V'SOSKE invented the hand-tufting process over 50 years ago. More recently, Roger McDonald, an extremely talented young interior-design-school graduate, has been inventing designs for these hand-tufted V'Soske rugs. His designs reflect the concerns and preferences of interior designers. Current collections emphasize interest in texture and in natural earth colors. In the group pictured McDonald mixes nature's straw beiges with red wines.

(Right) EDWARD FIELDS has patented a "Magic Needle" that helps a person to tuft pile from ⅛″ to 3″ in height with either cut or looped yarns. Fields' capacity for custom design is shown in his *Nature Collection* of ten rugs designed by talented Annie Sanders Bohlin. The collection dramatizes many faces of nature's beauty. "Shore Thing" will never wash away the writing in the sand. The "Forest the Eye Can See" captures the mystical magic of a walk in the woods at dusk. One gleans a glimpse of the summer moon half hidden behind pine branches. "Waves of Grain" suggests an airborne view of fecund fields. These and other Edward Fields designs are especially suitable for wall-hanging.

Furniture: Contemporary and Traditional

Good furniture of any period is a true reflection of its times. It uses the materials available and the technology of the times in an honest effort to answer the needs of society. Significant changes in furniture design come about when new materials are discovered, when new technologies are developed or when society has new needs.

Traditional furniture reflects the history of society through handcrafted techniques. Anything made before 1830 and the Industrial Revolution is, for sure, an "antique." (According to the U.S. Customs office, anything 100 years old is an antique, but some purists prefer to call only the handmades antique.)

The Industrial Revolution changed and confused everything. It bred a new moneyed middle class and provided it with the seeming luxury of machine-made mass-produced copies of the old aristocratic handcrafts.

Some sensitive people became disgusted with the monsters made by machine. They rejected the machine and sought honesty and integrity in the old handcrafts. Later, others realized that handcrafts were no longer a reflection of the times but that honesty was a good impulse. They tried to develop furniture of quality that was honestly machine-made. Hence, the Modern movement was born.

Bentwood
In 1840 Michael Thonet came upon the process of bending beechwood by softening it with steam. He bent the wood into continuous structural shapes to create chairs. Not only did he invent a technique; he was the first in the furniture field to develop a system of mass production. Thonet's designs became so popular that by 1921 his heirs owned twenty-one factories and employed more than twelve thousand people. Today you see Thonet's bentwood chairs almost everywhere—in countless restaurants, cafés and homes.

Tubular Steel
The Bauhaus School was set up in Germany in an effort to bring together art and technology and address their combined resources to answer the needs of the day. Marcel Breuer studied at the Bauhaus and became master of its furniture workshop. While there he was inspired by the handlebars of his bicycle to invent the first continuous tubular steel furniture frame. By 1929 Thonet Industries were mass-producing Breuer-designed chairs. Other architects—Stam, Mies van der Rohe, Le Corbusier—also realized the resiliency of tubular steel and created designs that seemed suspended in space. Instead of resting on four legs, seats were "cantilevered," supported only at one end by the continuous frame.

Molded Plywood
Molded plywood is nothing new, particularly in Scandinavia, where everyone knows about skis. However, Finnish architect Alvar Aalto realized that this material was strong enough to support cantilevered seating. He designed chairs of Scandinavian white birch that paralleled the tubular steel chairs in Germany.

American inventor Charles Eames designed molded plywood splints for the armed forces during World War II. He then developed molded plywood and metal furniture that won prizes at New York's Museum of Modern Art.

Wood
Danish designers Hans Wegner and Finn Juhl worked wood into sculptural forms. The quality of their craftsmanship has had a constant influence on modern design.

Plastic
Eero Saarinen felt that solid wood furniture was of the past; he preferred to work with man-made materials. A cast plastic pedestal forms the base of his graceful dining table and chairs, manufactured by Knoll.

The Italians are really responsible for exploring the possibilities of plastic in furniture design. (See pages 40–41.)

Systems Save

Systems design divides a total unit into its component parts. Instead of a conventional three-seater sofa, you might have three seats lined up to look like the standard sofa. Instead of a huge built-in bookcase, you might have stacking units that combine to create the same look. Creations of components allow flexibility of use, and they are easier to take with you when you go.

(Above) TURNER imports several "furnishing systems" from Germany's Behr factory. A collection of panels, adjustable posts and rails can be instrumental in furnishing complete rooms. Large expanses of wall can be converted into storage areas, entertainment centers, work areas by specifying shelving, drawers, flat surfaces, doors, swing-out bases for TV, cocktail bars, etc. Open space may be divided into activity areas by Behr walls—floor-to-ceiling, see-through or walk-through. The Behr 1600 group pictured saves space horizontally as well as vertically. The seating area is lifted a level so that slide-out beds may be stored underneath. Behr surfaces come in six different wood grains, including walnut and oak.

(Left) ATELIER INTERNATIONAL offers "The Software Seating System" designed by Mario Bellini and manufactured in Italy by Cassina. Basically, "Software" is a collection of interchangeable panels and fixed components that can be arranged to form chairs, beds, sofas and modular seating. Made of welded steel and polyurethane foam, the panels are attached to each other by industrial-grade zippers sewn into the panel covers.

Modular Is Movable

1

Part of the popularity of contemporary styling is certainly due to modern mobility. This is a country with a lot of get-up-and-go. When we move, we want our furnishings to make the move with us. Modular furniture moves, adapts, readjusts, rearranges—saves us from spending so much money all over again. Even if we stay put and become restless, modular furnishings can be rearranged to adapt to our moods. Today we don't want furniture to structure our lives and tell us how to behave; we want it to adjust to us. (Left) BAKER FURNITURE has been best known for the quality and caliber of its traditional period reproductions. Recently the company has brought its excellent care and craftsmanship to bear on a comprehensive *Modern Collection*. Made up of modules, the *Modern Collection* expresses the "needs and demands of today's mobile society," according to Phil Kelly, president of Baker.

Created by a clever young designer from Britain, Brian Palmer, the collection is incredibly adaptable. Amply proportioned modular seating units include corner and armless sections and ottomans. Storage units can do almost anything. What do you need? A bar, a desk, a bookcase, a TV or stereo cabinet, a cabinet with closed-door storage, drawers? Twenty-two different modules can stack up to serve your needs. Made of fine woods such as bird's-eye maple and Macassar ebony and accented with simple steel hardware, the modules can create storage, shelving, entertainment centers, free-standing room dividers, even rooms-within-rooms. The 18″- and 36″-wide stacking units can be locked together at any of three heights. This makes it possible to create bridges and spans, pass-throughs and see-throughs. (What a terrific big boy's toy!)

There are straight-edged units and rounded elements. The rounded elements may be used to turn corners or to create scallop-edged rows of shelving. Repeating the circular theme are round tables that may be used individually or wedge-locked together to form a cluster coffee table. Easily movable on hidden casters, the tables offer interior storage space. Thinking of everything; Baker offers compatible furnishings to complete an interior.

2

1. FOUNDERS shows a stacking drawer system and a companion modular seating group. The drawer system is in the new neutral of the late 1970s, gray—in a lacquer finish. The compatible upholstery is shrimp with gray, a fabric design created by Sarina Mascheroni and manufactured by Cohama.

2. ERIC LAUREN is a new designer source for contemporary furniture. The company shows modular seating systems upholstered in fabrics from Jack Lenor Larsen. Occasional tables complete the picture.

3. THAYER COGGIN has long been a leading manufacturer of contemporary furniture. Milo Baughman is the designer who has kept the company in the forefront of design. Current collections of seating are modular and designed with comfort the first considera-tion. In this setting the same fabric is used as upholstery and as a frame for the window. (Such a structural frame around the window is called a "lambrequin.") The fabric is designed by Sarina Mas-cheroni and manufactured by Cohama.

3

Furniture Is Designed to Save Space

Today more and more activities are being jammed into smaller and smaller spaces. More and more people like the clean, simple look of contemporary styles. How can manufacturers accommodate all those activities while still seeming simple? Dual-purpose sleep-sofas are an answer. Vertical storage systems are another. Manufacturers are inch-pinching in corners and other unused areas.

1. SIMMONS' "Baldwin" Hide-A-Bed sofa and companion ottomans provide ample seating and restful sleeping space.

2. AVERY BOARDMAN shows a chic day bed, upholstered in an Alan Campbell fabric. Quicker than a yawn, the day bed can convert into a generous double bed.

3. SELIG shows a setting with ample answers. To save space one sofa is a sleep-sofa; stools tuck under the table. To expand space

a mirror is hung over the table and the coffee table is glass. To seem simple, everything coordinates with the colors of the upholstery. To achieve the "eclectic" look, the comfortable contemporary sofas are upholstered in a traditional fabric.

4. KELLER WILLIAMS breaks up the boxy look of a room by establishing seating on the diagonal; but no space is wasted as the triangular corner becomes a storage area.

(Right) NAOMI GALE makes the most of valuable vertical space. Vertical systems for storage and display can be wall-hung or free-standing, in styles from Mediterranean to modern—all custom-designed to hold what you have.

The Influence of Italy

Italian furniture has been very well received in the American marketplace. It all began to happen in the late 1950s and early 60s when Italy stunned the world with a tremendous wave of new ideas about furniture. At that time the American design elite was devoted to the purity and functionalism of the Bauhaus school of thought. Many Americans rejected those forms and furnishings as forbidding, cold and sterile.

Then came the Italians. Not by nature cold or sterile, but rather warm, exuberant, sensuous and playful, the Italians developed designs that answered our yearning for comfort and luxury. Shapes were curved, comfortable, often joyous, sometimes humorous.

How did it happen? The Italians discovered the possibilities of plastics. Plastics could be molded into free-form shapes. Rigid conventional structures need no longer limit the imagination. Italian imaginations went to work. Designers and manufacturers explored new technologies and applied existing technologies to the fabrication of furniture. For example, they used an injection-molding machine (made in the U. S. in 1964) and made the world's first injection-molded furniture in 1969.

To the comfort of soft, squishy cushioning they added the luxury of butter-soft leathers and suedes, creating simply sinful (and irresistible), sensuous seating.

They played with Pop Art for fun. They scaled up an apple in a hat and made it into a seat. They scaled up a bird's nest with eggs to create an environment for a human to cuddle up into.

They developed modular wall storage systems—perhaps because Italian homes have no closests, or perhaps as an outgrowth of their creation of compact kitchens.

Italian manufacturers gambled on gifted designers to propel them to success, and they did. American importers serving the design trade started bringing back innovative Italian designs.

In 1972 more Americans became aware of Italy's excitement at a show called "Italy: The New Domestic Landscape" held at the Museum of Modern Art in New York. The show was in two parts. One was an elegant shopping orgy, showing the flowing forms of the new plastic technology, shocking and/or amusing Pop Art objects, materials of perfectly lascivious luxury and wonderful workmanship. The other part of the show was the opposite—restrained, contained environments for living that were anti-object, just down to the discipline of the no-nonsense necessities. Such minimal multiuse environments were mobile and unwasteful of the world's natural resources.

It's clear: We loved the luxury and comfort. We were also titillated by the truth that possessions can become obsessions that burden, rather than brighten, our homes and hearts.

Today much more Italian furniture is imported, or manufactured under license here. Many Italian furniture manufacturers have their own showrooms and outlets. American manufacturers have been stimulated by the Italian success to copy their concepts (if not the details of their designs). Instead of all these derivative designs, American product designers wish that American manufacturers would be encouraged by the Italian example to trust the taste and judgment of America's own innovative designers.

(Left) CASTELLI's "Plia" chair has had an enormous American success. Designed by Gian Carlo Piretti, the sleek and simple steel-framed chair folds flat to take up a very small storage space. Now in addition to transparent plastic, seat and back are offered in cane.

(Right) SAPORITI ITALIA opened a showroom in New York (called Campaniello Imports, Ltd.) and almost immediately had to expand. To house many of his new furnishing designs, Giovanni Offredi created an atmosphere of plush, calm sophistication. Some of his new designs include seating groups with removable arm segments for easy reupholstery, steel-framed chairs that can be stacked for storage and designs of diverse textural treatments. An example is shown: a columnar concrete base supports a cruciform shape of stainless steel that supports a floating glass tabletop.

1

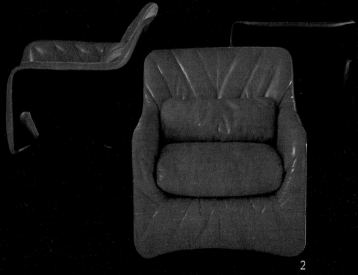

2

Plastic Promoted
Sculptural Shapes

Americans were using plastic for industrial parts. It had advantages. The material was lightweight, strong and amenable to molding. The physical structure of some plastics was stronger than structural steel. Molded shapes of single-piece construction saved the production processes and costs of creating structural joinings.

The insightful Italians took this technology and applied it to the fabrication of furniture. Not only did plastic make industrial sense; it made aesthetic sense. Plastic freed furniture forms from the rigid right angles of conventional construction. Suddenly there was an outpouring of fluid furniture forms—sculptural shapes in hard, smooth plastic or soft squishy polyurethane foam.

Lightweight hard plastics had their own advantages. For the first time in furniture, color was intrinsic to the material. It couldn't wear or chip off. Smooth, slick plastic surfaces were tough and easy to clean—in fact, childproof.

Plastic foam furniture was engineered in different densities to create the utmost comfort in seating. Soft fluid forms took the edge off abrasive days.

Plastics technology revolutionized the furniture field, giving birth to joyous sculptural shapes.

1. ARTEMIDE is another innovative Italian manufacturer that has found fortune through fine designers. These molded chairs, designed by Vico Magistretti, are made from fiber glass-reinforced plastic. The easy-to-clean durable designs are available in a pretty palette of colors: pure white, fresh green, rich chocolate and now beautiful burgundy. For fun, table legs match. Several of Magistretti's designs are on permanent exhibition at New York's Museum of Modern Art.

2. BEYLERIAN imports furnishings from the Italian manufacturer Arflex. The sculptured seating shown is designed by Carlo Bertoli and is made from a molded shell padded with polyurethane cushions wrapped in Dacron. All is upholstered in leather or COM (Customer's Own Material).

(Right) TURNER has found excitement in European centers other than Italy. From the Artifort factory in Holland, the Turners import Pierre Paulin's well-known seating sculptures. Several have won awards here and abroad. Two out of the dozen chairs shown are on permanent display at New York's Museum of Modern Art.

Although neither molded nor plastic, the cocktail table pictured is a sculptural shape. The table has an oval glass top cantilevered from a marble base. Its designer, Ronald Schmitt, was discovered by the Turners at the Cologne Fair in 1972. "Everything he makes is a piece of jewelry," they state. Truly, these furniture forms are art.

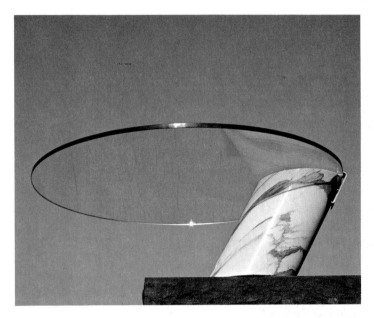

Back to Nature

The back-to-nature movement has had a number of inspirations. It was the kids who wanted to live in their jeans and "tell it like it is" and move to farms. It was the people fed up with the city who longed for country air and innocence. It was the oil crisis that made us realize that our natural resources are limited and that we had better preserve what we have. It was also the oil crisis that reduced the availability of plastics (a petrochemical product) and encouraged a return to wood (even in Italy). It was Nixon's trip to China that began the importation of Chinese brooms and baskets. Designers began to use a lot of baskets in interiors, and from there they began to use an occasional piece of wicker, rattan or bamboo. They found that its natural, earthy texture mixed well with either contemporary or traditional styles and that its light look worked well in small spaces.

Now rattan, wicker and bamboo are no longer classed as a seasonal summer look, and many manufacturers are making furnishings of these materials—or furnishings that look as if they are made of these materials.

CASA BELLA offers the *Vivai del Sud* line of bamboo and wicker furniture made in Italy. The bamboo frames of "Sambu" (above) can be color-matched with fabrics, such as the green tones of the patchwork pattern pictured. (Vivai del Sud fabrics are designed by Valentino.) The Vivai shell chair in wicker is as cozy as a cocoon for one or two. It has a companion chaise.

Back to the Past: Antiques and Reproductions

Today traditional styles are being mixed with modern to create the "eclectic" look. Designers aren't as rigid about style purity as they once were. They realize that old pieces give poignancy to modern interiors, that the mellow tones of the old provide a pleasant contrast to sharp, slick or architectural modern. Perhaps it was the designers' clients who caused the "eclectic" look by refusing to be parted from their old family treasures. Most people want part of their past with them in their life in the present. And those people who don't have part of their past to bring along usually want to buy a piece of the past.

Those who have homes with traditional interiors sometimes want additional furnishings to blend with the style they have. What should they buy?

Antiques or Reproductions?

Whether one buys an antique or a reproduction depends on two things: time and money.

Assuming that it even exists, an antique with the right look will take time to find. You and your designer will have to scout and search. Reproductions are readily available. They may even be in stock—ready for delivery.

Antiques are *not* always more costly. Astounding as it may seem, the original may cost only a fraction more, or maybe less, than the reproduction manufactured with today's high costs of material and labor. If you are buying furniture as an investment, consider carefully the antique. If it is truly representative of the time in which it was created, well crafted and purchased at a sensible price, the antique will most probably appreciate in value over time. As soon as you get it home, the reproduction will become a piece of second-hand furniture and will lose value at a rate depending on how fine a copy it is. Of course, if the original doesn't exist, or is prohibitively expensive, the reproduction is the sensible choice.

How can you get value for your money?

First of all, the piece must "work" in the room, otherwise it's not worth whatever you pay for it. The traditional styles that are popular today are the ones that can adapt to our living circumstances.

Because today we live in smaller spaces, the small-scale styles of the past, such as Louis XV and XVI, are popular. Those that bought these French 18th-century antiques in the 1930s and 1940s have realized an astronomical increase in the value of their acquisitions. Large-scale styles are out of place today. Those that bought large-scale Gothic and Renaissance antiques at the height of their popularity in the early 1900s are hard put to find a market for them now. Reproductions of these styles are made in smaller sizes.

The Bicentennial awakened our awareness of our past. People have been visiting restorations and enjoying the timeless elegance of 18th-century furnishings. Many would like to live with fine furnishings like those they have seen. American 18th-century antiques have had an incredible price rise in the last ten or twelve years. However, English 18th-century antiques, on which most American is based, still offer great possibilities for purchasing and profit, even though prices have doubled since 1970. The Bicentennial inspired many manufacturers to create collections of 18th-century American reproductions. Some collections were supervised by historical societies to guarantee authenticity.

We like the back-to-nature or country look. The simplicity of Shaker furniture is enormously appealing. Painted pieces with the naïve designs of country folk art are attractive. Simple furniture of solid woods creates a country mood and is sturdy.

Because manufacturers have realized that we like soft, cushy comfort they have revived the overstuffed styles of the 1920s and 30s. Original pieces from the 20s and 30s aren't old enough to be antiques, but prices are inflated because they are popular.

Our interiors are becoming more simple and architectural. German "Biedermeier" and English Regency are two antique styles that are suitable to such modern design schemes. Both styles are small in scale, architectural in character and good buys today. English Regency also has some Egyptian influence—an influence that is growing in popularity.

To get value for your money, it is important to buy styles that suit your space. With antiques it is best to buy a style just before it comes into fashion. (A designer is a better advisor than your local gypsy.) In any case, avoid buying a style at the height of its popularity and expense.

The piece must be authentic and of good quality.

Antiques must be "valid," or true to their time. For example, an Impressionist painting painted today is not valid. The Impressionist era is not now. If in the past your grandfather had bought a painting from Van Gogh to save him from eating his paint tubes, the work would be valid, a true reflection of its time.

Reproductions as a generalization are not valid; they are copies of somebody else's era. With a reproduction you get the most value for your money if it is an "authentic" reproduction, perhaps endorsed by a historical society (such as Kittinger's *Williamsburg Collection* and Baker's *Historic Charleston Collection*), or made by a firm with a fine reputation (such as the English reproductions made by Wood and Hogan), or at least true to the originals you've seen in museums. Avoid buying reproductions that are themselves antique. You will be paying for age, without getting the original.

The piece must have high-quality materials and craftsmanship. With an antique it is not enough to be old. A lot of junk dates from the golden age of the Renaissance.

(Left) BAKER FURNITURE has introduced the *Historic Charleston Collection,* more than 40 reproductions of the fine furniture from the great Georgian and antebellum mansions of Charleston, South Carolina. The Charleston Historic Foundation initiated this program of reproductions with Baker Furniture in order to generate royalties for the preservation and restoration of its landmarks. The finely crafted and authenticated collection includes designs from the Queen Anne, Georgian and Regency periods. The collection reflects the ultimate in 18th-century elegance from a town once considered the richest city in the New World.

Each item will make its history known to the purchaser through hang tags identifying the cabinetmaker who made the original piece, the house it came from and the nature of the design.

PART TWO
Designer Interiors

Why Hire a Designer?

Me? Hire a designer? You're crazy! Designers are just for rich people. Besides, I want my home to be me. I don't want anyone telling me what I should like!

So goes the refrain. Hiring a designer is an unthinkable thought to a lot of people. But think of it. Times have changed.

Interior Designers are not just for rich people.

If designers are just for the rich, consider the fact that there aren't so many rich people as there once were. Consider the fact that today there are many more interior designers than ever. The American Society of Interior Designers has 7,000 student members alone. These are people who want to set themselves up in the design business. And there are already about 38,000 designers in practice! Clearly, there aren't enough wealthy people to go around. Even if designers didn't want to, they would have to work with people of more moderate means. They are.

Interior Designers can help you express your personality.

Of course you want your home to reflect your individuality. Of course you don't want somebody sashaying in telling you how to live. You're right. Hiring a designer doesn't mean denying your individuality or lifestyle. It just means finding someone who knows how to translate your lifestyle into furnishings, fabrics, colors, styles and shapes.

The conception and creation of an interior design (with or without an interior designer) is absolutely dependent on your input. A good interior designer will try to get to know you and the other members of your household well enough to interpret your own desires. You have the right to approve or disapprove anything he suggests. The designer wants to please you. After all, it doesn't improve a designer's business to have discontented clients. The word gets around.

A Designer can actually save you money.

If a designer is good for nothing else, he can save you from making expensive mistakes. Wouldn't it be awful to lay down $1,500 for a sofa only to get it home and find that it's too big for the room or that it clashes with the rug? A good designer will take responsibility for how things look together. He is trained to be able to visualize the finished effects in advance.

Designers plan. They don't operate by trial and error. You might learn a lot about design principles through the trial-and-error method, but why go to the agony and expense? Why be forced to live with an expensive mistake you can't afford to replace? Why not avoid risk and learn what works together by asking your designer to explain his plans?

Designers can help you get value for your money. They can anticipate your future needs and select furnishings that will adapt. They know what will wear well and what looks you'll love more and more the longer you live with them. They know how to breathe new life into your old furnishings. Wouldn't you feel frustrated to spend money on a carpet that wears out too soon, or on a painting that soon becomes tedious? Wouldn't you like to find some clever way to make use of what you have?

Through an independent designer you might be able to purchase merchandise less expensively than through a store. Ask a designer how he charges. He might charge a fee for his time and let you have merchandise at the wholesale price, or as his fee he might charge a percentage above the wholesale price. You might do better than the 100 percent or more mark-up in a retail store. Not only do you get a bargain for your money but a design service as well! On the other hand, at a quality furniture or department store you may have the privilege of charging.

A Designer will work within your budget.

He might try to get you to spend more money. Fair enough. You can say no. Some designers will give you an hour's consultation for a fee. Some will take small jobs—even so small as a commission to frame a couple of pictures. You don't need a mansion and a monstrous budget to talk to a designer. They're not a breed so proud that they won't take work. If a designer is so busy he can't take on the job for you, there's another one out there who will.

The way to get the best work out of any designer is to be honest with him. Tell him exactly what you want to accomplish and what you want to spend. This will define his challenge. If he can't deliver what you want for the price, he's got to tell you up front. If you're not direct and honest, the designer won't know what he's up against, and everything might end in disappointment for everyone.

A Designer can save you time and aggravation.

Do you actually know how to articulate space, shape, color, texture and lighting to create the effect you would like? Do you actually know where to buy all the furnishings you wish you had? Do you have the name and phone number of a painter, a wallpaper hanger, a refinisher on the tip of your tongue or on the top of a file card? Do you actually have the time and inclination to get after manufacturers for mistakes or late deliveries?

Why not leave the aggravation to the experts? Designers know how the parts of the puzzle fit together. They know where to find what they want to buy. They know who offers the best service for the money. They have clout with manufacturers because they are constant customers.

Designers are creative, not weird.

Some people dismiss designers by just calling them weirdos. How weird is it to have imagination? What would life be without it? Everywhere you would see the same sterile solution to the same predictable problems. Designers are selling their inventiveness, their ability to come up with solutions that aren't the same trite old clichés. New ideas, new solutions brighten our lives, give us fresh energy, save us from boredom. Designers are masters of the unexpected twist. They can find "that special something" that gives a room the spark of life.

Designers can cope with reality.
Designers can work with what you've got—your family, your furnishings, your psychic set. Designers suffer from the reputation of being too idealistic, of not understanding why you won't part with your favorite chair. If a certain designer won't work with your favorite chair, you can hire another who will. Just tell him what he's up against. _Open - honest._

Designers are teachers.
Some people are afraid of designers because they know nothing about design and they don't want to be made to feel stupid. Why should you assume you should know everything about design? Do you know everything about dentistry when you go to the dentist? Do you know everything about tax law when you go to an accountant? No, you go to the expert because he is one and you're not. Like any other expert, the designer will identify your problem or problems and tell you the possible range of solutions so that together you can decide on the best course of action.

The problem of interior design is psychologically loaded because your home is such an immediate reflection of your identity. People will come into your home and judge what kind of person you are. Some people are afraid to expose themselves to that judgment. It's scary if you don't know how to manipulate the elements of design in order to represent yourself well. And if you hire a designer, it's scary if you can't visualize what he is suggesting for you. Maybe you won't feel at all at home with what he does.

A designer is responsible for making you understand his suggestions. He should show things to you and explain things to you so that you clearly understand what he has in mind. You should never accept his ideas without understanding them. Feel no shame to ask questions. Not only will you learn; you are more likely to get what you want!

Some people aren't able to express in words the feeling or look they'd like to live with. It is the designer's responsibility to draw you out, to feel out what you might like. Then he will show you pictures or sketches of what he has in mind and you can react to those. Your reactions will help clarify the path he should take.

Truly, the designer/client relationship is one of mutual education. He is getting to know you and you are getting to know how you might express yourself and the life you like through design. Consider the remark of one satisfied customer: "The house is everything I've ever wanted but couldn't have conceived of until now."

Good design isn't something for somebody else.
Good design isn't a luxury; it's a way to enhance everyday life. Doesn't sunshine on the window sill cheer you? Doesn't a gay bouquet of flowers make you feel good? Essentially good design is the art of arranging your home to make you feel good—body and soul. Don't you owe it to yourself to hire a designer and enhance your life?

Designers Have Imagination

An Egyptian-Frescoed Flat

Who: Designer David Doolin
Where: His own apartment on Telegraph Hill in San Francisco

Photographer: Thomas Brooks

The Problem:
How to give oomph to an ordinary apartment.

The Solution:
Designer Doolin painted Egyptian frescoes on the walls.

At the time that David Doolin was doing up his flat, California had already caught the craze for ancient Egypt. Of all the fads that fascinate, ancient Egypt would not, at first, seem a promising premise for contemporary decor. But it did to designer David Doolin.

He studied the frescoes of ancient Egypt and set out to duplicate them in his apartment. To begin, he needed a wall surface that would suggest stucco. He found it in a rough-textured paper that is usually used as an undersurface in the installation of linoleum. That's a good eye for texture! Next he needed paints. He purchased Fuller latex paints mixed in shades to approximate the seven Egyptian colors: terra-cotta, brick, faded moss, pale blue, gray, and white, with apricot for background.

Next came his tremendous talent. He started in the dining area, copying and interpreting the frescoes from Abu Simbel and other ancient tombs. Bare walls he draped dramatically in white canvas. Slowly the canvas diminished as Doolin worked his way with paintbrush down the passage into the living room and the sleeping niche (taking time out now and then to paint similar frescoes for other designers and other projects).
He underplayed the rest of the apartment, not to compete with his wonderful walls.

The floor is a simple stretch of sisal. The furniture is minimal. Sofa and bed are built in on platforms. Dining table and chairs are spare modern. Lighting comes from wall-hung Luxo lamps.

The coffee table is an eye-stopper, and it reiterates the Egyptian theme. Doolin painted it to complement his walls and topped it with mirror to reflect his artistry.

Sources:
Cesca chairs: KNOLL. *Wall-hung lamps:* LUXO. *Paint:* FULLER.

DESIGNERS HAVE IMAGINATION 51

An Eclectic Mix in a Stretched Space

Who: Designer Michael Vincent, ASID
Where: His own flat on Telegraph Hill in San Francisco

The Problem:
To give piquancy and a fresh point of view to what otherwise might be a conventionally correct or routine apartment.

The Solution:
Vincent emphasized and expanded the sense of space.

He unified adjacent areas. He underscored the spatial flow from dining area to living room to study by giving all the floors and ceilings the same continuous treatment. The floors are an extended expanse of bleached and polished oak, and the ceilings are all pale pink lacquer trimmed with a polished chrome bullnose molding. The pale colors expand the sense of space, and the molding creates a line that draws the eye along its length, seeming to stretch the space.

Windows are all treated in the same skinny-slat polished chrome Levolor Lorentzen blinds. This light-looking, reflective and repetitious treatment unifies the all-over space and makes the most of the light.

The end wall of the dining area is mirrored, reflecting more light and air and depth and distance.

Furniture blends into the background, so it seems to disappear visually. The living-room sofa practically matches the walls. The dining-room table is similar in color to the floor.

The rooms are not crowded or cluttered. Many decorating devices conspire to create an airy, open feeling.

Vincent chose an adventurous variety of styles.

Because color contrasts are minimal, Vincent was able to combine a wide variety of styles without creating a jarring effect.

The dining chairs are 1920s reproductions of Chinese Chippendale, covered in white canvas. The dining table began as an ash plank over a steel base, but to soften its industrial look and to make it a mellow mix with the chairs, Vincent wrapped the metal base with macramé, achieving a look a bit like bamboo. He then painted the base white to match the chairs.

The chaise in the study is a Napoleon III 1860s copy of a Louis XVI design. Its refined and polished texture contrasts dramatically with the rustic bent-twig chair in the living room, but the two are in blending beige colors.

Vincent sparked the space with a large Corinthian capitol, circa 1910, retrieved from a local fish shop, and placed between the windows. A sculptured head (from 25th dynasty Egypt) eyes the area from the dining room. Both are in calm colors that are easily integrated into the space.

Rough and smooth are at play again with a six-foot Edwardian crystal vase in the dining area and a huge prickly cactus in the living room. The two are placed on the diagonal to balance each other. They harmonize because of their similar size. Something in common makes dissimilar objects integrate.

Photographer: Thomas Brooks

Sources:
Blinds throughout: LEVOLOR LORENTZEN. *Vinyl wallcovering/upholstery:* J. H. THORPE.

Inspired Irreverence and Soaring Space

Who: Architects and Interior Designers MLTW/Moore-Turnbull
Lighting Consultant—Richard Peters
Where: House in Westport, Connecticut, sited on a peninsula
in an estuary off Long Island Sound

Photographers: Photo right, Ezra Stoller
Photo left, John Fulker

The Problem:
To design a home that is at once fun and elegant and that takes advantage of the water view.

The Solution:
The architecture plays up the view and creates a sense of spaciousness.

The architects oriented the major living spaces—living room, dining room, kitchen breakfast nook—to face the water. They endowed the living room and the dining room with an air of elegance by letting them soar to two stories in height. The luxury of variety is provided by interspersing smaller closed spaces with the open ones. A cozy low-ceilinged seating space surrounds the living-room fireplace. A low-ceilinged area separates the living room from the ascending ceiling of the dining room. Other living areas are connected to the ends of the central space on the diagonal. The diagonal line is repeated on the stairway down to the dining room. Diagonals are dynamic—they lead the eye to explore the space that is beyond view. This adds adventurousness to the architecture.

In the interior, spaciousness and glitter give an elegant ambience.

Taking its inspiration from the water view, the window wall is covered in a pattern of fish scales. These solid areas glisten like a decked fish in the sun. They are spray-can-stenciled in silver and gold to give a glamorous glitter to the room.

The luxuriously large size of the space is emphasized by big pictures hung high on the walls and washed with light. Furniture is kept low or light.

In the dining room the chairs are light-looking, the table see-through and the storage pieces reflective stainless steel—all enhancing the spacious statement.

Funky furniture makes for fun.

Moore-Turnbull's houses always have imaginative furnishings devised by Moore himself and by his young associates.

At first glance, the living-room coffee table looks like ordinary oak, but look again. It is painted with patterns that look like spilled-over reflections from the fish-scaled wall. Mary Ann Rumney applied her artistry to an ordinary old Mission oak table.

In the guest bedroom (pictured) Larry Linder piled a collection of 1930s chests, dining buffets and drawer elements into an absurd sculpture and then integrated it all with the wall by painting a dramatic supergraphic over everything. This recycled furniture is a new experience. Its irreverence is refreshing. The large-scale size of the painting gives architectural éclat to the room. For fun the supergraphic theme is played out on the twin beds opposite. Painted headboards and bedspreads are variations of the theme. One is orange and rounded in shape; the other is blue and squared in shape. The opposites challenge each other—but they are really playful partners. It's all in fun.

Sources:
Living room: sofas, pillows: custom made by THE HOMEMAKERS CORNER, *West Haven, Conn. Carpeting throughout woven to order by* UNITED CARPET, *Westport, Conn. Corbusier chairs:* ATELIER INT.
Dining-room chairs: LAVERNE. *Guest bedroom lamps:* HANSEN.

Designers Can Fit Your Ages and Stages

Child's Play

Who: Designer—Noel Jeffrey
Client—Young New York couple with two small children
Where: A New York rental apartment

The Problem:
Not enough space for the children to play.

The Solution:
The couple took over a tiny studio apartment next door.
Since the space is rented, designer Jeffrey made no structural changes beyond creating a doorway between the apartments.
Jeffrey transformed the small space into an upbeat playroom by painting bright colors in graphic patterns.
Children are known to need floor space for romping and roaring about. Jeffrey knew he would have to do with the minimum of furnishings. How to make a place feel furnished without furniture? Color and pattern are the answers.

The color should be bright. Children are known to be stimulated by bright color—it is even supposed to improve their IQs. And what kind of pattern do you put in a small space? Diagonals on the floor seem to push the walls away and stretch the space. Jeffrey developed his diagonals and then filled in other areas with color. He shortened the long vista of the corridor by breaking it up into various color zones. He conceived a completely supergraphic space, with designs on the floor echoed on the ceiling and connected by the walls. The room is a graphic experience in 3D, enveloping and exciting.

The designer dramatized his color zones with light directed from ceiling tracks. Ceiling-mounted lighting is a good solution to a child's area because it is out of the way of play.
Other furnishings are child-supportive.
Acrylic panels hung from the ceiling not only help to define the graphic color areas; they also seem to lower the ceiling to child-scale.

The powerful paint job is protected by a coat of polyurethane, so everything is easily wet-washed.

The few furnishings are simple and sturdy. They include modular seating and an architect's work table.

Accessories are chosen for child's play and ultimate education. They include painted numbers, alphabets and geometric shapes. A blackboard and a bulletin board allow the children room for self-expression.

Photographer: Christopher Danes

Sources:
Seating: DAVID EDWARD. *Venetian blinds:* LEVOLOR LORENTZEN.
Track lighting: LIGHTOLIER.

Growing Family Relationships

Who: Architect—Charles Tapley, CTA Architects
Interior Designer—R. H. Wilson, Jr., of CTA office
Clients—A family with four children
Where: A heavily wooded, one-acre site on Houston's
Buffalo Bayou

Photographer: Hickey-Robertson

The Problem:
1. To design a home that will reflect the family's contemporary living style without stripping them of their traditional Southern heritage.
2. To provide the family with places to group together and places to get away from each other.

The Solution:
Timeless nature is emphasized.

Avoiding a conflict between traditional and contemporary, the architect emphasized timeless nature. The home is set in seclusion amid the foliage; its architecture is unobtrusive. Large windows encourage integration of the interior with the outdoors. The interior designer brought in the warm browns and refreshing greens of the tree scene in his color scheme.

There are rooms to get together and rooms to get away.

The living room, lounge and garden/game room provide a variety of spaces for groups to gather—large include-everybody groups or just-my-gang groups.

The dining room, too, encourages a variety of relationships. It is a long room, divided by a passage. The room's shape dictated two tables, each seating six comfortably. The family can all sit together, or its members can regroup with guests. This might even be a place to get away and study quietly. Reference books are handy in the wall-storage shelves. (The blue bar is a barrier to a stepped-down level.)

Upstairs, the master suite is separated from the older children's room, but the nursery is close by. The nursery is conveniently designed with removable walls so that it may eventually be converted into a study.

The guest room is isolated from the family quarters, allowing the guests the luxury of perfect privacy.

Comfortable furnishings combine contemporary with traditional.

The dining room combines the pedestal table by the modern master Saarinen with chairs styled after the 18th-century master Chippendale.

The living room combines sensuous modern Italian seating with a classic carpet and an exotic lacquered coffee table.

The garden/game room combines a modern Knoll chaise with time-defying bamboo furnishings by Ficks Reed. (Neither will be aged significantly by energetic children.)

Sources:
Living room: Seating: AI INTERNATIONAL, *made by* CASSINA. *Patterned rug:* ROSECORE. *Kashmir lacquered red coffee table:* LOYD-PAXTON, *Dallas. Dining room: Pedestal tables:* KNOLL. *Dining chairs:* KITTINGER; *fabric:* JACK LENOR LARSEN. *Garden/game room: Bamboo table and chairs:* FICKS REED. *Chaise:* KNOLL. *Floor matting:* ALISON SEYMOUR.

Acknowledging the Children's Adulthood

Who: Designers—Architect Donald D. Powell and
Designer Robert D. Kleinschmidt, both associated with
Skidmore Owings & Merrill in Chicago
Client—A prominent couple and their almost college-age
son and daughters
Where: A house in Springfield, Illinois, designed in 1962
by St. Louis architect Charles King.

The Problem:

1. To update the house to acknowledge and incorporate the young adults' life patterns into the active social life of the parents.
2. To make the house adaptable to changes in the seasons.

The Solution:

Changed and rearranged furniture fits the family's altered activities.

In the update, the living room was to change from a formal reception room into a family living area. However, on occasion it would still have to entertain the parents' peers at parties for political causes or benefits. (At these times the children could beat a civilized retreat to the library in the other wing of the house.) A large squared-off U-shaped sofa provides luxurious lounging for family as well as seating for many guests. Completing the conversational group, and providing a pleasant contrast to the squared shapes, are rounded armchairs on either side of the fireplace. A two-seater sofa at one end of the room is the center of a secondary seating group. On the end opposite, a card table and chairs are placed for family fun.

In the dining room, the designers wanted to create an intimate atmosphere for family as well as for guests. They had three problems to overcome: the ceiling seemed too high; the room seemed too noisy; and the door to the kitchen seemed distracting. To lower the ceiling, a ceiling panel hung at a 10-foot height within a lighted cove was painted a dark terra-cotta color. To absorb sound, the designers wrapped the walls with insulating material

and then covered them with natural beige linen. To eliminate the distraction of the swinging kitchen door, they set up a folding screen and upholstered it in the same linen as the walls.

The former library was to be recast as a family business and entertainment center, incorporating desks, lounge seating for relaxed reading, a piano and stereo equipment. The room was blessed with a wooden storage wall incorporating a fireplace. The stereo equipment was naturally placed in the storage wall. The sofa was naturally placed to face the fireplace—a position perfect for stereo listening. Desks were cleverly used as sofa end tables, saving space and creating a clean continuous long line with the sofa. The piano was placed opposite the entrance to brighten the vista from the hall.

The master bedroom was replanned to accommodate the family's happy habit of gathering together for intimate talks before breakfast and in the evening. The designers provided a warm, soft, rearrangeable environment with five modular seating units upholstered in wheat chamois, punctuated with pillows of fox fur.

Natural materials and neutral/natural colors reflect the family's more sophisticated outlook.

The designers developed an integrated color scheme for the whole home, inspired by the colors of the architectural materials. The house was built with terra-cotta brick and mortar of a mustard/putty color. The living room featured a teak wood-paneled wall and a large fireplace made of travertine. The teak wall seemed similar in color to the terra-cotta brick, and the travertine fireplace seemed similar in color to the mustard/putty mortar. Here was a color theme that could integrate the whole home, inside and out.

The teak living-room wall is part of an architectural box that encloses the dining room. The designers decided to define the other outside walls of this box with the terra-cotta color. To unify and harmonize the house, they determined that all other interior walls, plus the exterior siding and soffits, should be painted the mustard/putty color. They varied their basic color throughout the home in order to compensate for differing lighting conditions. For example, on the darker north side of the house they lightened the paint so the rooms would seem sunnier.

Keeping consistent, most floors are covered with a Berber wool carpet that is two shades lighter than the walls. However, for the sake of easy maintenance, the floor in the entry is complimentary cork, and the floor in the dining room is oiled teak. Window treatments in all rooms blend into the mustard/putty/beige background. Furnishings, too, carry through the theme in shades of bronze, terra cotta, rust and beige.

To make visitors feel warm and welcome, the designers broke out of their restrained scheme in the guest room. They splashed bright yellow paint over one wall and wrapped the bed in bright blue. All in an effort to greet a guest with excited enthusiasm.

The designers built in seasonal variety.

The living-room sofa is upholstered in bronze mohair. This rich, warm color combines with the U-shape of the sofa to create a cozy sense of enclosure during the winter weather. In the summer, the sofa wears a linen cover the same color as the carpet. It then blends into the background to create an open airy space. In the master bedroom, the twin beds are covered with quilted beige flannel in fall and winter and light-looking natural linen in the summer. Bolsters remain a dark plum-eggplant color, but three separate sets of pillows allow color play. Artworks throughout the house are changed with the seasons.

Sources:

Front entry: Cork floor: KENTILE. *Kilim rug:* MARIAN MILLER. *Bench: architect-designed, fabricated by* LAKESIDE FURNITURE MFG. CO.

Dining room: Wall upholstery: HENRY CALVIN LINEN (*acoustical fiberglas behind fabric*); *installed by:* HOMECRAFT DRAPERY AND UPHOLSTERY CO. *Table:* DUNBAR/DUX. *Chairs: rebuilt and restyled by architects; stained and upholstered by* LAKESIDE FURNITURE MFG. CO.; *upholstery:* AMERICAN LEATHER "CALFSKIN."

Living room: Carpet: ALIKART "PITYPANNA" *from* CARSON PIRIE SCOTT & CO. *Sofa: architect-designed; fabricated by* LAKESIDE FURNITURE MFG. CO.; *upholstery:* KNOLL INTERNATIONAL. *Love seat and lounge chairs:* WARD BENNETT DESIGNS; *upholstery: Himalayan Goat by* AMERICAN LEATHER. *Drum tables: fabricated by* LAKESIDE FURNITURE MFG. CO.; *upholstery:* AMERICAN LEATHER. *Coffee tables: architect-designed; fabricated by* STEMBRIDGE MFG. CO. *Draperies:* BEN ROSE. *Card-table chairs upholstered in natural horsehair:* ARTHUR H. LEE & SONS.
Library: Lamps: HARRY GITLIN. *Sofa and ottomans:* JACK LENOR LARSEN *fabric. Flower vase on desk, ceramic ashtrays:* TIFFANY & CO.

Guest room: Built-in shelf/desk unit: fabricated by WOODWORK CORP. OF AMERICA. *Bed: architect-designed; fabricated by* LAKESIDE FURNITURE MFG. CO. *Upholstery:* BRICKEL ASSOCIATES. *Headboard and pillow upholstery:* AMERICAN LEATHER, *chamois. Stool:* KNOLL INTERNATIONAL; *upholstery:* KNOLL "CAVALIER." *PVC slat blinds:* LOUVER DRAPE INC.

Master bedroom: Chaise: fabricated by LAKESIDE FURNITURE MFG. CO.; *upholstery:* AMERICAN LEATHER, *chamois. Bronze drum table: architect-designed; fabricated by* LOUIS HOFFMANN & SONS, *Milwaukee. Coffee table in front of chaise: architect-designed; fabricated by* STEMBRIDGE MFG. CO. *Beds and bedspread fabric:* KNOLL INTERNATIONAL; *bolsters:* JACK LENOR LARSEN *fabric. Beds, spreads, pillows: fabricated by* DELTA WORKROOMS INC., NEW YORK. *Draperies:* BEN ROSE. *Vertical blinds:* LOUVER DRAPE INC. *Vase on coffee table:* TIFFANY & CO.

All paints: MARTIN SENOUR

Florida Retirement for Fun

Who: Architects and Interior Designers—Charles W. Moore
Associates
Client—A busy historian and his family
Where: Captiva Island, Florida

The Problem:
To build and furnish a home for the client's future retirement.

The Solution:
Moore made the most of the climate.

The architecture is designed to confuse the distinction between inside and outside; inside and outside interpenetrate. The house consists of two L-shaped units that wrap around a central garden. The units do touch, but literally only at one point. The bases of the L shapes are bent or carved out so that they *just* touch and outside space enters between them. The center picture above shows the meeting point. A continuous floor and enclosing glass walls make the point into a passage. Architect Moore wanted to give a person the sensation of going outdoors when walking from the living room to the dining room.

The fireplace is also given a tricky treatment. It is set outside the house and connected with glass spacers. Light comes slipping in between the fireplace and the house. The fireplace may provide warmth in the winter, but its icy glass isolation prevents it from being an oppressively hot symbol in the summer.

The glass-walled gazebo off the living room (above left) seems disconnected from the house. The wall that does in fact connect it to the living room is painted green and lighted from the side. Both the color and the light serve to seem to push the wall away. Again, one has the sense of going outside.

The interiors are cool.

Floors are slick, cool vinyl asbestos tile. But Charles Moore didn't leave it at that. Thinking "cool," he thought "water," so he laid the tile in a pattern of radiating ripples moving out from the focal-point fireplace. Bands of solid and checkerboard tiles spread out in square waves of concentric circles.

New furniture is cool, crisp white—upholstery plus plastic pieces. The white provides a refreshing clean contrast with the family's old favorite furniture (and sets off its mellow mood).

Contrast to the cool comes in punchy pillows and pictures in hot hues.

Sources:
Living room: Wicker sofa: DEUTSCH. *Caster chairs:* SELIG. *Small tables:* DOOR STORE. *Wicker table:* WALTER'S WICKER WONDERLAND. *Moroccan rugs:* ERNEST TREGANOWAN. *Dining table:* J&D BRAUNER, INC.
Kitchen: Plumbing fixtures: AMERICAN STANDARD, KOHLER, ELKAY, ELON. *Dishwasher and disposal:* KITCHEN AID. *Wall oven:* THERMADORE. *Refrigerator:* GENERAL ELECTRIC. *Range:* CORNING. *Washer and dryer:* GENERAL ELECTRIC. *Locks:* SARGENT. *Hinges, hardware:* STANLEY.

Photographer: James V. Righter

Designers Can Help You Express Yourself

Anything Is Possible— Even the Extreme

Who: Designers—Denning & Fourcade
Client—Fashion designer Diane von Furstenberg
Where: A New York apartment in a 1920s building of early
fireproof construction with ugly beams in the ceilings

The Problem:
To please a very individualistic client.
The Solution:
The designers had to figure out what she wanted.

Robert Denning explains his approach: "Listen carefully to what your clients say. Then sift and try out a room. For Diane, we began in the bedroom.

"There's a great sexuality that she likes in her clothes and whatever she does—even her decorating. The idea of the way it feels, the kind of pinkness it gives in the look . . . Her look is very sex-oriented."

The designers also discovered that Diane is attracted to the exotic. For example, she likes the symbolist paintings of Redon.
The designers sought to create the sexy, exotic look she liked.

The living room consists of three conventional conversational groupings—a sofa and two chairs gathered around a coffee table. But there's where convention ends!

The sofas are a voluptuous Deco-like style—superscaled rounded shapes, with soft skirts and button-tufted bolsters, with outsized pillows added. The chairs are Turkish Victorian. "When we found that Turkish Victorian furniture we found the idea for her apartment—the *orientaliste* look that she liked," explains Denning.

Over the major conversational grouping hangs an Andy Warhol triptych portrait of Von Furstenberg. Its jarring Pop palette of colors is used muted for the rest of the room.

The sofa is colored in skin-flattering tones of peach and apricot. The material is unashamedly sexy satin. The exotic Turkish Victorian corner chairs are covered in an India print fabric.

The seating is set against a background of glowing gold. The floor is covered with an antique Aubusson carpet of gold with wine. The walls are not only gold; they are upholstered in fabric to make the room feel sexier and softer. Pattern on the walls, as well as on the chairs and floor, gives the room an *orientaliste* richness.

Overhead, the ugly beams are painted a peach-orange against blue-gray ceiling panels, tones that work well with the walls.

In the entry hallway a Russian runner laid on existing wall-to-wall carpet leads right into the exotic interior. On the way, the walls are paneled in mirror alternating with smoked acrylic sheet. The acrylic ceiling is set within a lighting cove, which sets the scene a-sparkling.

The bedroom is frankly feminine, all soft and pink. Walls and bed are upholstered in the same peach-patterned fabric (an idea that softens the sharp architectural angle behind the bed). The lilac of the pattern's flowers is picked up on a sensuous silk velvet chaise. The ugly beams and all the other woodwork are harmonized into the scheme by being painted in the compatible color mauve. The flushed floral fantasy is brought down to earth with a warm deep-brown carpet. A bamboo étagère and table have an appropriate light look.

Whatever you have to say about this apartment, it *is exotic* and *sexy*. The designers delivered what the client wanted.

Photographer: Norman McGrath

Sources:
Living room: Sofas: GUIDO DE ANGELIS. *Satin apricot upholstery:* STROHEIM & ROMANN. *Coffee table: antique. Floor lamps: antique, 1905. Fringes and cording:* STANDARD TRIMMINGS. *Wall and furniture upholstering:* EMMANUEL SIDLER. *Wallcovering:* & VICE VERSA. *Turkish furniture: antique; upholstery:* CHINA SEAS.
Entry: Burgundy mottled vinyl wallcovering: WOLF-GORDON.
Bedroom: Wall fabric: dress fabric (discontinued). Mauve silk velvet upholstery on chaise: SCALAMANDRE. *Bracket lamps:* GEORGE HANSEN.

DESIGNERS CAN HELP YOU EXPRESS YOURSELF

A Male Intellectual Makes the Most of His Space

Who: Designer—Gerald Allen, an architect-trained critic and co-author of The Place of Houses *with Charles W. Moore and Donlyn Lyndon*
Where: His own apartment in a renovated brownstone in New York City

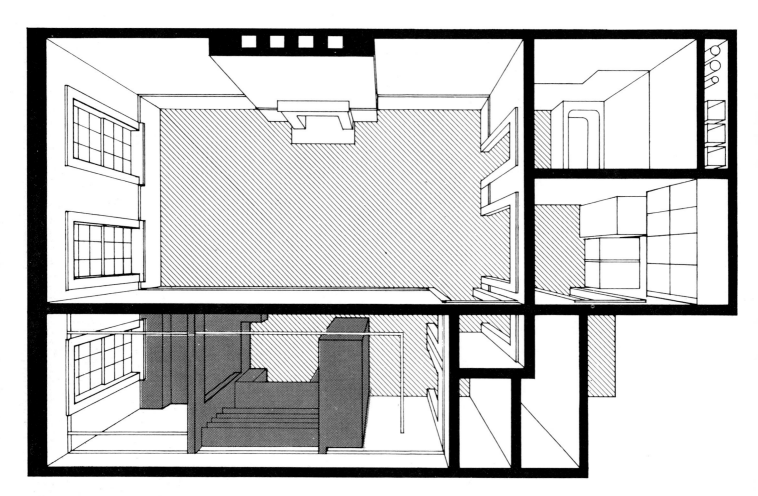

The Problem:
1. To separate areas for different functions within a tiny space.
2. To create a joyful environment for himself.

The Solution:
A skylight painted on the ceiling separates the areas for conversation and dining.

A fool-the-eye painted square skylight on the ceiling of the living room defines the conversational circle, around which tables and bar equipment serve dining and drinking. Separate rugs in each area also help to delineate the difference.

A room-within-a-room in the bedroom defines spaces for dressing, studying and sleeping.

(See plan above and next pages.) To begin, Allen had a long boring bedroom. In it he wanted to dress, sleep, study and store a lot of stuff. He devised an ingenious solution by building in a structure that would not only break the room up into three separate areas but also *create* storage spaces.

As one enters the bedroom one is faced with a half-width red wall. Part of the wall has inset shelving containing audio equipment and musical scores. The other part is a hanging surface for pictures and a mirror. This half-wall faces the closet and thus defines the dressing area.

Walking by the red wall, one enters the study. A desk top supported on file cabinets fits between red walls. Above the desk are storage shelves up to the ceiling. The back of the flat part of the entry wall also offers storage up to the ceiling. To improve the proportions of this milk–carton–shaped space, Allen hung an 18th-century Dutch brass chandelier to lower the view.

The study opens into the sleeping platform. Actually the sleeping platform extends out into the study area to offer a storage space for architectural drawings. A shelf under the window by the bed provides a place for books, control panels and TV. Lighting throughout the space is provided by a plug-mold ceiling strip.

Allen symbolizes the things he loves to create a personal and joyful environment for himself.

Allen loves music, architecture and literature, and it makes him happy to surround himself with references to these things.

A wall-hanging of felt over the sofa is an allusion to architectural history. It looks like an architectural arch of heavy stone, but since

Photographer: Gerald Allen

it was initially designed as a window curtain, the stones are amusingly tied back like conventional curtains.

It may be too subtle to see, but the living-room walls are painted in a series of stripes—some narrow, some wide, some painted in flat paint, some rendered in glossy paint. The organization of the stripes creates for Allen an analogy to the rhythms of music—something that gives him pleasure without intruding on his guests.

Over the fireplace Allen enjoys a literary pun from James Joyce: "For a burning would is come to dance inane." Allen is making fun of the fire—its wood and flames.

Allen's allusions may be a bit esoteric for most of us, but the important thing is that he enjoys them and they make *him* feel at home. He believes ". . . you need to know what you *care* about—and draw upon those things to make a place to live, whether it's an apartment or a house . . . [whether it's] cheap or expensive."

Fitting a Couple's Sizes, Habits and Interests

Who: Interior Designer—Gere Kavanaugh
Architects—Kahn, Kappe, Lotry & Boccato
Client—A couple of vastly different sizes
Where: A beach-front condominium in Los Angeles, California.
The house is designed with wide columns
that rise through all levels.

Photographer: Elyse Lewin

The Problem:
1. To find furnishings to fit a couple of opposite anatomies. He is six two; she is a petite five feet.
2. To accommodate what they do comfortably.
3. To express their interest in Japan.
4. To design the interior to harmonize with the architecture.

The Solution:
Seating is custom-made or carefully chosen for comfort.

The male client likes to read while stretched out on a sofa. To specify a suitable sofa, the designer measured the man horizontally and also the width of his arms. Extra inches were added to make the man comfortable and to suit the size of the living room's two-story space. A 106-inch-long sofa with 8½-inch-wide arms was ordered in a pair so that sofas could face each other across the fireplace and repeat the symmetry of the architectural columns.

For occasional seating in the living room and for lounging in the library the designer searched for and found commercially available seating that both clients found comfortable. The occasional chairs and the dining chairs are the same style, so it is easy to pull up extra chairs for a feast.

A huge desk provides work space for both husband and wife.

Both husband and wife enjoy working in the early morning. Designer Kavanaugh created an 18-foot by 3-foot glass work table that spans the width of the upper-level library (left) to allow both ample work space with seaside vistas. An interesting sidelight of this solution is that the desk fills a building code requirement for a horizontal guardrail at the open loft level.

Stereo cabinets under the glass top are placed so that sounds abound for good listening in the living area below.

Both sides of the architectural columns seem the same, which helps the harmony.

The interior is infused with oriental accents.

The client has business and travel interests in Japan, and many of the furnishings reflect this. The black, white and wood interior is accented with red lacquer. Red lacquer turns up on the finish of the Prague bentwood chairs, on the stereo speakers and on the custom-made light fixture above the dining table.

The Japanese method of layering lacquer—up to 25 coats—is not only used on the speakers and light fixture but on the dining table, the book shelves and all cabinetry.

Accessories are predominantly oriental. The couple's art collection consists primarily of Japanese prints, and the large handsome hanging in the living room is a collage of swatches from antique kimonos. A Noguchi paper lantern hangs in the hallway. Decorative pillows feature patterns of oriental influence.

Sources:
Draperies: ISABEL SCOTT. *Bentwood chairs:* STENDIG. *Plastic tables:* BEYLERIAN. *Custom furniture fabricators:* VAL'S CABINET, DAVE EDBERG, KASPARIAN, B. WOOD SANDERS. *Lighting custom fixture in dining room:* GRUEN LIGHTING. *Standing lamps in living room:* LIGHTOLIER. *Plants:* MARGOT SMITH.

A Place for Parties

*Who: Interior Designer—John Dickinson of San Francisco
Client—People who enjoy entertaining
Where: The living room of a handsome house designed by
architect Julia Morgan (of San Simeon fame) in
San Francisco's Presidio Heights*

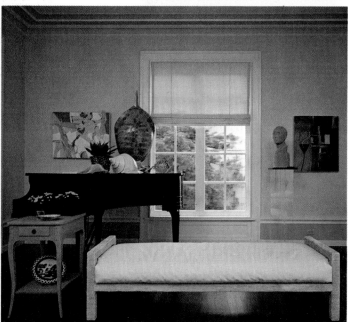

Photographer: Jeremiah O. Bragstad

The Problem:
The client wanted the living room redesigned as a special place for entertaining. (When alone, the family prefers the cozier library.)

The Solution:
The interior is inspired by the architecture.

Architect Julia Morgan's post-World War I work is characterized by strong architectural detailing and symmetrical settings. Approached from the redwood-paneled entrance hall, the doorway to the living room is expressive of this style. Designer Dickinson decided to play up the architecture by underplaying the interior.

Opposite the entrance is a handsome bay window. To welcome the incoming guests, Dickinson wanted to place a sofa under the windows. He custom-designed one to reiterate the shape of the bay.

In front of the sofa he wanted a rug that would repeat the same three-sided shape—symmetrically. He ordered an octagon. On opposite sides of the centered rug Dickinson positioned backless benches. On the angles off the entrance he placed pull-up chairs. The shape of his scheme is clearly inspired by the architecture.

Not to detract from the room's architectural excellence, Dickinson made the furniture blend into the background. Furniture, rug and walls are white. He made the window treatment hang within the frame. His choice of Roman shades is simple and architectural.

Walls are painted white in a matte finish. For emphasis, woodwork is lacquered glossy white. Handsome ceiling moldings are painted in subtle bands of chamois, pearl gray and pale apricot (colors that are also picked up on the sofa pillows).

The interior is inspired by the requirements of a pleasant party.

A large party requires lots of empty floor space for guests to mill around and for tray-laden waiters to circulate and serve. The central space is kept clear. Furniture sits at the edges of the rug. Beyond the central area, off the rug, there is more open floor space. One can get off to the side by the piano or by the fireplace. The backless benches allow one to face either way to talk.

A pleasant party has fresh air. An excess of smoke and hot air (verbal or physical) is a drag. Designer Dickinson's all-white scheme is crisp and clean. But Dickinson did more. He brought in the air of the country with rustic knotty pine "packing case" coffee tables. These rustic tables also emphasize the refinement of the architecture by setting up a startling contrast.

At a pleasant party guests feel coddled and cared for. What could have a more luxurious and lavish look than an all-white room? How impractical! Surprisingly, not so. The material that Dickinson has chosen for sofa, benches and blinds is an extraordinarily silky Belgian cotton canvas that is so tightly woven that would-be-disastrous spills can be washed or brushed from its surface. But for sure security, Dickinson supplied a second set of removable covers.

Sources:
Upholstered furniture fabrication: HILDEBRAND. *Packing-case table fabrication:* RANDOLPH AND HEIN. *Canvas:* MERCIER ET FILS. *Rug:* INTERNATIONAL FLOORCOVERINGS.

The Look Is "Ours" As Well As "His"

Who: Interior Designer—Angelo Donghia, ASID
Client—Young couple with three lively children
Where: An old coach house on an estate in Deal, New Jersey,
used as a summer house and a frequent winter retreat

Photographer: Masaru Suzuki

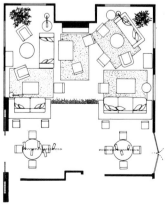

The Problem:
1. Making the most of the old coach house.
2. Adapting the designer's "look" to suit the family's casual and sociable life-style.

The Solution:
Donghia emphasized the assets of the old coach house and minimized its liabilities.

What Donghia loved was the light. Large light-flooding windows. And the setting. Facing barn doors open on one side to a beautiful tree-shaded walkway and on the other to a pleasant pool house.

What he didn't like was the unsuitably shiny floor and the dark ceiling beams. He wanted the whole interior to look light and speak of sunshine without creating a blinding shine.

He stripped the floor and pickled it. Unlike the kitchen dill drill, pickling the floor entails sanding, bleaching, rubbing with an oil-base white paint and sealing. The finished effect is light, almost white. Walls and ceiling (including the beams) were painted white to open up and air out the interior. Donghia spread the sunshine.

To take advantage of the view out the big barn doors, Donghia placed dining tables on a raised platform by the doors. This was almost an inevitably deduced decision. The kitchen is adjacent, complete with a convenient pass-through, and the shape of the platform is so long that the choice of two tables seemed sensible. Perched on the platform, the dining tables have the added advantage of an overview of the seating space.

Donghia wanted to harmonize the platform with the seating space and create an architectural integration with the facing fireplace. He cut out the platform to create space to insert sofas. He left an empty center space that repeats the exact width of the chimney breast opposite.

Relaxed sociability is encouraged by an unbelievably flexible furniture arrangement.

The seating area is anchored at the end by the inset sofas, in one corner by a rounded-back armchair and in the other corner by a small sofa set on the diagonal. Other seating allows incredibly flexible social interaction. The open-sided chaise allows seating in any direction. Small armless chairs can be turned to join one conversational group or another. Small striped rugs define social centers, but one need not toe the line.

The interior is distinctly "Donghia."

The clients hired Angelo Donghia because they like his "look." They got it. Donghia used his own furniture designs and his own fabrics (from his famous firm, & Vice Versa). The major fabric was inspired by the circular painting hung over the fireplace. Donghia admired the painting so much that he asked its artist, Richard Giglio, to do an adaptation of the design for fabric. The print is used in profusion—on the plumply pillowed sofas, on chaise and armchairs. Bright and busy, it adds to the happy relaxed mood of this holiday home.

Sources:
Additional sources beyond the DONGHIA *furniture and* & VICE VERSA
fabrics include: Round coffee/tea table: BIELECKY. *Woven cotton scatter
rugs:* ROSECORE.

Showing Off a Collection

Who: Architect—MLTW/Turnbull Associates
Client—Collectors
Where: A standard 1930 woodframe house in Palo Alto, California

Photographer: Rob Super

The Problem:
1. Not enough space. The client wanted a small addition built onto the house—a new study downstairs with a loft bedroom above.
2. To showcase the clients' collections of Pre-Columbian, African and Asian art and artifacts.

The Solution:
The architect built an ingenious addition.

He built out to the property line in front of the house but kept the addition secluded from the street by avoiding windows. The front facade is rough-sawed boards with only a door to let the outsider in. As we all know, being shut out makes a person curious. The lack of windows adds to the suspense (and to the surprise)

when a guest does enter. The architect feels it serves to underscore awareness of the owners' fine collections.

Turnbull positioned the new front door in line with the length of the house. By this device he opened up a vista extending 55 feet from the entrance (photo right) through a small intermediate room (the old foyer) to the end of the living room and out through the rear windows (photo top center). The long vistas provide an emphatic visual contrast to the clusters of small art objects that invite close scrutiny.

As well as providing the needed space and emphasizing the artwork, the architectural addition orchestrates spaces that give new life to the boring bungalow. The outside may be closed, but the inside is open. Once in the door, one has a great sense of space. There is a skylight overhead and sliding glass doors to the side. This same open motif is repeated on the other side of the addition in the study. In the center there is a second story containing the loft bedroom. The differences that are introduced in shapes, sizes and ceiling heights between the new and the old serve to sweep away the deadening sameness of the 1930 layout.

Interior architecture is designed for display.

Turnbull created continuous pillow-piled seating platforms with stepped ledges for plants and objects. He devised a series of plywood boxes of different sizes, all painted white, to serve as changeable, stackable units for display and storage. These neatly tailored and simple solutions become background. Their simplicity sets off the intricate and interesting art.

Sources:
Cesca and Wassily chairs: KNOLL. *Hall bench:* GEORGE NAKASHIMA. *Palaset storage, fabrics:* DESIGN RESEARCH. *Hardware:* SCHLAGE. *Paint:* FULLER. *Plastic skylight:* FILON. *Aluminum windows, doors:* FENTRON.

Living Carefree with a Collection

Who: Architect—Fred Briggs
Interior Designers—The husband-and-wife team of
Lloyd and Suzanne Faulkner
Client—California Collectors
Where: A tree-shaded lot on a harbor in Newport Beach, California

Photographers: Wayne Thom and Fritz Taggart

The Problem:
1. To design a home to take advantage of the super setting.
2. To express the clients' easy-living lifestyle and to display their special treasures.

The Solution:
The house is open to the outside and open in the inside.

Architect Fred Briggs oriented the rooms toward the water or toward the trees. The beauty of California country is kept in view. Space flows not only from inside to outside but from room to room. Living areas are open and airy. Rooms flow into one another, and the living room is a two-story space. Light is let in not only with sliding glass doors but with a series of skylights.

To stand up to the super setting, the architect chose strong materials for the interior shell. He used natural red brick and resawn cedar.

The interior designers took their cue from the spectacular sunsets and the interior architecture.

They chose a rich red color scheme to underscore the impact of the sensational sunsets over the sea (and also to blend with the brick). They chose strong, simple furnishings to stand up to the impact of the interior space. They brought in plants to echo the outdoors.

They played on the architectural theme of skylights in the dining room by cutting an octagonal shape in the ceiling, boarding it with cedar planks and then bordering it with lights.

They created a custom table for the clients' collection.

Designer Lloyd Faulkner created a clever display for the clients' collection. It is totally visible and accident-proof! Objects sit in individual lucite cylinders on an illuminated surface, under a removable tabletop.

Sources:
Carpeting throughout: WESTWOOD CARPET CO. *Living-room seating:* METROPOLITAN *in* KNOLL *fabric. Lucite table: fabricated by* GREG ASHCROFT. *Pillows: fabricated by* VIRGINIA FOUST. *Bar chairs:* LAVERNE. *Bar top: fabricated by* FRANK ROHLOFF. *Dining buffet tile top:* INTERPACE.

A Historical Hobby Sets the Style

Who: Architect—Ralph E. Schaefer
Interior Designer—Ernest Lo Nano
Client—A history buff and his family
Where: suburbs of Milwaukee, Wisconsin

Photographer: Bill Engdahl, Hedrich-Blessing

The Problem:
To reproduce the traditional grace of a plantation house built along the James River in Virginia about 1780.

Natives of Wisconsin, the family had spent several years in the Washington, D.C. area, soaking up Revolutionary history, visiting the museums and historic houses of Maryland and Virginia and haunting the local antique shops. At the same time, they began to collect 18th-century furniture and store it in a barn. By the time they returned to Wisconsin, their dream was a house that would reproduce one of those they had seen on the James River.

The Solution:
They hired appropriate experts.

They commissioned architect Ralph Schaefer, who had done several fine traditional houses in the area, to design a two-story red brick Georgian house with a center entrance and wings at each end.

Inside, the architect designed fireplaces and Chippendale-style paneling and moldings based on those of such Virginia plantation houses as Stratford Hall, the birthplace of Confederate General Robert E. Lee. To simulate the combed plaster of old houses, he had the white walls plastered unevenly, painted heavily, then brushed. For floors, he chose traditional random plank in oak, stained mahogany.

To complete the interior design the clients turned to Ernest Lo Nano, a New York antiques expert and consultant to Colonial Williamsburg, Inc.
Designer Ernest Lo Nano combined their collection of antiques with authentic reproductions and fine old oriental rugs.

"In each room," the designer explains, "we started with the rug, taking colors from it for woodwork, drapery and upholstery fabrics." The living room (left) reflects its striking blues and deep pinks from an antique serape, woven in the Heriz district of Iran. In the dining room (right) the Persian rug, a Fereghan, covers the plank floor with a color range of sage, coral, blue and beige. The woodwork and paneled wall are sage, the chair seats coral and beige.

In the living room antiques and reproductions are in happy harmony. The sofa, side chairs and tea table pictured are reproductions by Ernest Lo Nano Interiors. End tables are antiques. A mahogany drop-leaf George II card table is at the side of the sofa by the fireplace; a Queen Anne mahogany birdcage tilt-top pie-crust table is at the other end. Balancing the sofa across the room is an antique mahogany William and Mary secretary. All accessories are antiques except for the wall sconces, which are reproduced by Lester Berry of Philadelphia.

In the dining room, all the furnishings are antique. The mahogany dining table, made in England about 1820, is served by mahogany Hepplewhite chairs from a set of 12, also English, circa 1780. A Federal bow-front chest, circa 1800, is a Salem original. The finest antique in the room is an American mahogany sideboard, with serpentine front, circa 1795, which is beyond the right of the photograph.

Accessories include: on the Federal chest, a satinwood lace box, English, circa 1790; over the chest, a mid-18th-century oil with antique frame; and over the fireplace, a mirror, made in Scotland about 1800, with a carved walnut-and-gilt frame and brass candleholders. On the dining table, a Chinese export bowl in the rose medallion pattern, circa 1820, holds tea roses.
Accessories are underplayed.

Designer Lo Nano and his clients managed to resist filling the rooms with a clutter of unnecessary and inappropriate accessories. The effect is spare, restrained, dignified and authentic. "The rooms you see in museums are usually filled up with a lot of little things, because curators like to show their collections," Lo Nano observes. "But inventories of household possessions in the 18th century show there weren't that many things about at that time."

Sources:
Sofa, wing chair, tea table, side chairs: reproduced by ERNEST LO NANO
INTERIORS. *Dining-room chairs upholstery:* BRUNSCHWIG & FILS.
All other upholstery: SCALAMANDRE. *Lighting reproductions:* LESTER
BERRY, *Philadelphia. Oriental rugs:* GABRIEL RUG COMPANY.

A Man on the Move

Who: Interior Designer—Peter Andes
Where: His own apartment in New York City

The Problem:
In his own apartment, the designer wanted to express his belief that today's furniture should be portable, flexible, minimal.

"Because people are more and more mobile and cannot spend unlimited funds each time they move, I think our furniture must be modular. This is the way things are going to be in the future," predicts Andes. Andes' credentials lend extra credibility to his statements. He studied architecture at Yale, worked with the Knoll Planning Unit and was project designer on Mexico City's lavishly elegant Camino Real Hotel.

The Solution:
Stacking elements are modular, movable, multi-functional.

Photographer: Norman McGrath

The seating is made from a system of stacking pillows that may be arranged and rearranged to the limit of invention. There are 30 stacking pillows, each 3-foot square, plus throw pillows that are 2-foot square. "In this room, which is 18 by 28 with 8'6" ceilings, I could put three 7-foot sofas," Andes explains, "but where could I use them again? With this system, not only can I move it anywhere and have it fit, but I can stack it up and set up drawing boards in the living room if I need to turn out a project in record time."

Other elements of Andes' stacking system include stacking plastic tables, stacking ashtrays and stacking chairs, plateware and glasses in the dining room. Andes' furnishings formula has proven its adaptability. It has already been moved three times.

In addition to its movable and multi-functional assets, the stacking system creates a distinct design identity through repetition. The repetition theme is also seen in rows of white plastic plant pots.

The no-color color scheme can go anywhere.

White and charcoal gray can fit any architecture while creating a basic background for people and events. Pillows are upholstered (by General Drapery) in men's suiting material, a favorite choice of Peter Andes. They blend into the background of the rug to make the space seem even more stunningly simple. "The principle," Andes states, "is to do everything as directly as possible."

Even though it may be moved, the design suits the space.

Although walls and ceiling are white, varying shades of white define different architectural elements.

The large scale of the pillows suits the large size of the space. "The pillows make the large space intimate by changing the scale," explains Andes. "When you look at the place, you assume that it is a normal room size, except that you know the 3-foot square pillows are making up a 12-foot sofa instead of a 7-foot sofa. And you find that when someone is sitting at the far end of the room, not only do they sound farther away, but they look smaller and farther away."

Designers Can Make the Most of Your Location

Serenity in the City

Who: Interior Designer—John F. Saladino, Inc.
Project Designer—Peggy Wong
Clients—People who happened to mention that they like ancient
Tuscan villas and would like to spend some time
in Tuscany, Italy
Where: New York City apartment with a spectacular view of
the East River and the Manhattan skyline

The Problem:
1. To create an environment to make the clients happy.
2. To make the most of the view.

The Solution:
Saladino took inspiration from the clients' feeling for Tuscany.

To dream about being in an ancient Tuscan villa is to wish for sunshine, serenity and space—a relaxing release from the pounding pressures of big-city living.
Saladino sculpted space.

In the entryway he covered the ceiling with reflective stainless steel. Mirroring the space below, the ceiling seems to double the height of the room, creating the illusion of an impressively grand space, not unlike the courtyard of a 16th-century Italian villa.

Designer Saladino made some architectural alterations in order to create inviting vistas. Opposite the entrance a rounded wall invites the eye to roll to the right or left. To the left, Saladino cut across the corner of the master bedroom to make space for a diagonal step leading to the living room. The step has the effect of extending the living room into an area the newcomer can see from the entry, thus offering him an invitation to come in and explore.

Saladino elevated the living room not only to provide variety to the interior vistas but also to gain an advantageous vantage point on the exterior view. The end wall is dominated by a window that shows a simply spectacular scene of the city. In addition to elevating the whole living room, Saladino further elevated a wide window seat to provide a perch for enjoying the bird's-eye view. And to allow the most unobstructed view possible, Saladino replaced the apartment's original windows with almost frameless ones.

Opposite the living room is the dining room facing north. It has a view, too, but Saladino opened up even another vista between rooms. The dining room opens on one side to the den and on the other to the breakfast room. Saladino provided sliding doors between the rooms to allow variable views.
Textures and colors evoke the Mediterranean sunshine.

The walls of all the public spaces—the entryway, the living room and dining room—have textured unbleached plaster walls in the Mediterranean style. Matching calm cream carpet and leather cushions in the living room are voluptuously, sensuously soft. Marigold cushions on wicker chairs and lilac velvet cushions suggest sunshine and flowers. The atmosphere enfolds like basking in the sun on a sandy beach. It is a soothing, sybaritic space.

Sources:
Entryway: Antique runner: THE PILLOWRY. *Storage drums:* INTREX.
Cabinetwork: NAVEDO WOODCRAFT CORP.
Living room: Sofas: SAPORITI. *Wicker chairs:* DEUTSH, DRAPERY
MODES *(fabric). Coffee table:* STENDIG. *Carpet:* EDWARD FIELDS.
Lamps: LCS INC. *Antiques:* JOSEPH RONDINA. *Upholstery:* FLAM
ASSOCIATES. *Window seat:* NAVEDO WOODCRAFT CORP. *(cabinetwork),* S. FARKASH INC. *(fabric). Painting by* ED KOERNS *from*
SACHS GALLERY.
Dining room: Granite dining-table top: DOMESTIC MARBLE & STONE
CORP. *Chairs:* HARVEY PROBBER, ISABEL SCOTT *(fabric). Tapestry:*
DORIS LESLIE BLAU. *Planting:* C. KIND & CO.

Photographer: Norman McGrath

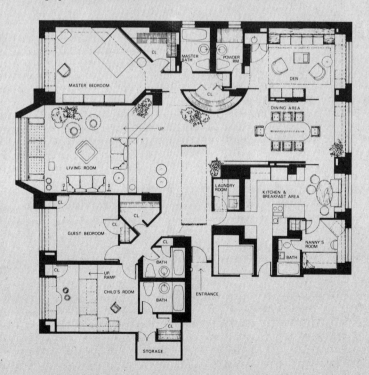

Avoiding City Sameness

Who: Interior Designers—Zajac and Callahan
Clients—People with rather traditional, somewhat
conservative taste
Where: The clients were moving from a historically detailed
townhouse apartment—with fine moldings and a chimneypiece—
into a new apartment house, well above average but
one still without details.

Photographer: Robert Perron

The Problem:
1. To give an ordinary apartment oomph and architectural interest.
2. To suit the clients' taste—to make the apartment "undecorated-looking" but distinctive.

The Solution:
A large Art Nouveau mirror gives the standard living room character and a sense of architecture.

The living room lacked all architectural assets. It had no fireplace. No view. Not even any moldings. The room needed a focal point and some dimensional definition. Designers Zajac and Callahan came upon an ornate Art Nouveau mirror, and (eureka) found the answer. "The mirror was so right and sensational for this room that we couldn't resist," confesses Zajac. They set the mirror above the sofa, and suddenly the room acquired an aura of dimension and detail. "The mirror has given character and architecture to a room that basically had none," Richard Callahan concludes.

An all-beige color scheme and a minimal use of pattern keeps the place looking cool, calm and conservative.

The browns and beiges of the mirror are repeated throughout the apartment. What could be calmer, more soothing or more conservative?

Contrast between shiny lacquerlike textures and rough woven-straw textures give the apartment individuality and éclat.

"Somewhere we had seen . . . Japanese red-and-black lacquer combined with woven straw," recalls Zajac. That combination gave the designers the theme that inspired their scheme. They designed a dining table with surfaces of woven straw and edging/detailing of red-and-black lacquer. Then the theme moved on.

Woven straw takes all types of forms. Split bamboo blinds at the windows. Woven wicker baskets from Madagascar for the plants. Chairs with caned backs for the dining room. Then there is a variation of the theme—we leave the straw but stay with the weave. The designers chose a rug in a basketweave design and a similarly styled quilted sofa upholstery.

The lacquer look provides punch in a red coffee table. The shimmer slides over walls and ceiling in glazed beige. Polished wood, crisp chrome, glistening glass, crystal and lucite lamps are other shining examples.

It is the textural tug of war between rough country weave and smooth city shine that gives this apartment its undeniably distinctive character.

Sources:
Sofa, stools, dining-room chairs upholstered by THOMAS DeANGELIS.
Fabric on stools, sofa: TRESSARD. *Bergère chair: reproduction. Table beside sofa: English Regency marble-top antique "scagliola," modern steel base:* JOHN VESEY. *Carpet:* ROSECORE CARPET CO. *Lamp:* HANSEN.

A City Center of Excitement

Who: Interior Designers—Edward Zajac and Richard Callahan
Where: Their own apartment in an upper East Side brownstone
in New York City

The Problem:
The designers wanted their own home to be simply sensational!

The Solution:
They treated ordinary architectural features extraordinarily.

The apartment began with a white Victorian fireplace, ordinary
windows and no moldings. Zajac and Callahan were not about to
be so mundane. They designed their own answers to the architecture. They wrapped the fireplace wall with wooden battens. They
covered the windows with exotic lattice screens (like something
they'd seen from Madagascar). And they designed a rustic twig-
like plaster molding to frame the windows, doors and ceiling.
These choices are wildly diverse in inspiration, but they work well.
The battens simplify the fireplace while creating a vertical line
that seems to stretch the ceiling height. The lattice screens let in
the light while concealing the view. The twig moldings provide
architectural emphasis and a country squire kind of sophistication.
They took their color scheme from a Baroque theater.

Red and gold set the stage. The traditional colors of a Baroque
theater inspire a sense of glitter and glamour.

"We wanted to make the apartment look as if it were terra-cotta,"
explains Zajac. He and his partner achieved a rich variegated red
in one weekend of work—with four washes of modeling clay,
acrylic glazes and clear acrylic. They spread their magic mixture
over walls, ceiling, window lattices and moldings.

The floor reflects the shine of gold. Over a rather standard
parquet floor Z&C superimposed a painted floor—a wood design
copied from a floor in Chopin's Warsaw house.

Various furnishings carry out the theme of gold glitter—the
Louis XIV marble mantel, the bleached pigskin Louis XVI chairs,
two tables and a commanding column with its even more commanding Turkish head.

Neutral gray is used to soothe the scheme. It appears in twin
tweed sofas and little lacquer stools designed by Z&C. It is mixed
with gold in the tiles of the fireplace surround and in a peaceful
painting by Julius Goldstein.

Once they had set the stage, they put on a play.

All parts of the room have roles to play; the excitement comes
from the interaction. The actor with the most powerful presence
is put on a pedestal. The waters seem to part in front of him,
driving a diagonal line through the room and causing furniture to
be sorted to its sides.

There is also drama of delicacy. A long table serves as the setting
for an eclectic arrangement of artifacts—Japanese ginger jars,
porcelains, sun-burst monstrances and flowers on a black-lacquered
table. All contribute in harmony to orchestrate a perfect triangular
composition.

Zajac and Callahan's is indeed a virtuoso performance! No
wonder they have achieved a formidable reputation among the
famous and fashionable.

Sources:
Stools and fire screen: Zajac & Callahan designs, made by SEGUIN MIR-
ROR & BRASS INC. Painting of floor: RICHARD NEAS. Upholsterer:
THOMAS DeANGELIS painting: by JULIUS GOLDSTEIN from BAB-
COCK GALLERIES.

MAKE THE MOST OF YOUR LOCATION

In a Small City Space Minimal Is Multi-Use

Who: Designer—Joseph D'Urso, known for working in a refined industrial idiom
Client—Reed Evins, an open-minded 20-year-old shoe designer of great visual sophistication
Where: A one-room apartment in Manhattan, featuring a 28-foot expanse of windows, providing sunshine and a view of the city skyline

Photographer: Peter Aaron

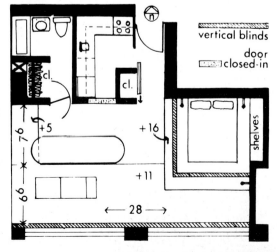

vertical blinds

door
closed-in

cl.

cl.

+5

+16

+11

28

The Problem:
1. To make the small space function both for daily living and entertaining.
2. To emphasize the view.

The Solution:
D'Urso made a positive of what is usually considered a negative.

Modern metropolitan high-rise buildings are made by stacking horizontal units up in a vertical mass. D'Urso used the stacking of horizontal platforms as the theme of his interior. He followed, rather than fought, the aesthetic of the building.

Under the windows a continuous 28-foot platform underlines the view, hides mechanical units and provides seating for a table.

At the east end of the space two shallow platforms rising 5 inches at a time are stacked under a mattress to form a separate sleeping area.

To give the room a sense of symmetry, another smaller platform—3 feet wide and 5 inches high—butts against the wall on the west side of the room.

He simplified the space.

D'Urso unified the walls. The wall opposite the windows was broken up by a doorway into the L-shaped kitchen and an opening into the closet and bathroom area. The designer smoothed out the surface by walling off the kitchen doorway and hanging an aluminum hospital door in front of the closet corridor. Then he finished all walls with high-gloss white paint to create a smooth, pure effect.

Floor and platforms are unified with a continuous covering of gray industrial carpeting.

D'Urso hung simple vertical blinds at the windows and around the sleeping area. He had the clarity of vision to see a parallel between the requirements for the window treatment and the requirements for the sleeping space. Both needed to open to an outside view in order to create an expanded sense of space; both needed to enclose in order to create a sense of seclusion and privacy. The vertical blinds allow manipulation of the view without much ado.

There are only three pieces of furniture. The mattress is one, and it seems to be a repeat of the platform concept. The table makes two. Resting on three sturdy steel columns, it is fixed in space like the platforms. At more than 10 feet long and 3 feet wide, it is large enough for any work project or party. Its surface is easy-maintenance black rubber and its edging is glittering, glamorous polished stainless steel. The third piece of furniture is a chaise designed by Le Corbusier. This classic of modern design has the purity of line to make it sympathetic with the simplified space.

Lighting is unobtrusive and functional. Track lighting and Luxo lamps give the owner flexible control of the lighting level.

The D'Urso concept is liberation through limitation.

The static space does not predetermine activity. "I try to create firm, clear backgrounds for my clients. Then they are responsible for giving them life," explains D'Urso.

Sources:
Carpet: CENTURY CARPET. *Lighting:* HARRY GITLIN. *Vertical blinds:* C.B.S. VERTICAL BLINDS. *Aluminum door:* ELIASON CORPORATION. *Chaise:* ATELIER INTERNATIONAL.

Synthesis with Sun and Sand

Who: Architects—Robert A. M. Stern and John S. Hagmann
Associated Architect—Alfred De Vido
Interior Design Consultant—Ward Willoughby of
Joseph Braswell Associates, Inc.
Where: A dull ranch house on a spectacular site on Long Island,
New York. The front of the house faces a busy street
(the major community route to the beach); the back of
the house has lawns that stretch right to the sandy
shores of the Atlantic!

Photographer: Ed Stoecklein

The Problem:

To remodel the house to take advantage of the sunshine and the seaside view.

The Solution:

The house was opened up to the view and shut to the street.

On the street side of the house the architects chose high, shallow windows to block the view but let in the light. On the ocean side of the house they reoriented the walls into large zigzag shapes with long windows in order to pierce the interior with sunshine and open it to vistas of the ocean.

To gain an advantageous perspective, they moved the major living area to a new second floor. Emphasizing the pleasures of gazing at the sea, they created a conversation circle in a shape suggesting a summerhouse gazebo. It is defined by an octagonal ceiling overhang supported by columns.

A second-story terrace is set on the diagonal to catch the morning sun. The master bath looks out on it and the ocean.

The interior makes the most of the light.

The interior brings in the colors of sand and sun. Floors, moldings and columns are bleached wood; walls are white-painted plaster. Furnishings in the conversation circle are sun-washed sand colors, plus a pale pastel print. The piano was bleached to continue the light look. By the piano, rattan and chrome chairs surround a burnt-red (sunburnt) game table.

In the downstairs dining room, the bleached-blond look flows from the floor to the oak table pedestals and the oak frames of the dining chairs, but in this room the designers are playing up the glamour and glitter of night light rather than sunlight. The table top is "Solarbronze" glass, and when lit by the overhead track lights, its surface shimmers with exciting reflections.

The furnishings fit the architecture and suggest airy ease.

In the dining room, the tabletop is boat-shaped to repeat the curve of the bay window. In the conversation pavilion, an octagonal rug repeats the shape of the ceiling. Furnishings fit in the angles of the octagon. The rest of the living area is spare and full of air.

In the master bath, a continuous sculptural form of reconstituted marble wraps around the exterior walls, encompassing a half-moon basin and a raised tub with steps. A mirror-lined vanity opposite the basin is carved out in a semicircular form to complement the curve of the basin. The bath with its ocean view is a sybaritic space that has all the lazy luxury of a serene summer.

Sources:
General: Lighting designer: CARROLL CLINE. *Venetian blinds:* LEVELOR LORENTZEN.
Living room: Sofas: custom-designed by JOSEPH BRASWELL ASSOCI-ATES, INC. *Sofa fabrication and fabric, custom chaise and ottomans:* FURNITURE SPECIALTIES. *Pastel print fabric:* CLARENCE HOUSE. *Custom coffee table:* KARL SPRINGER. *Side tables:* ROBERT WEBB. *Custom rug: fabricated in the Orient. Game table:* INTREX. *Game table chairs:* HARVEY PROBBER.
Dining room: Antique dining chairs: CLYDE WYBRECHT.
Bathroom: Reconstituted marble: VENETIAN MARBLE WORKS. *Marble floor:* COUNTRY FLOORS. *Vanity stool:* LUCIDITY.

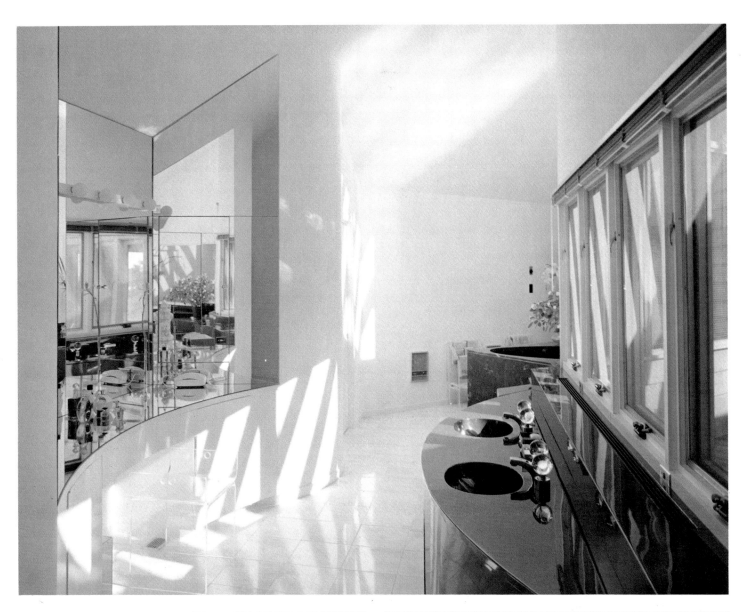

A Lighthearted Weekend Retreat in the Country

Who: Designers Anthony Tortora and Jay Crawford, co-owners of Quadrille Wallpapers, Inc., a stylish design showroom in New York City
Where: A charming salt-box-style house in Long Island, New York, to be used as their own weekend retreat

The Problem:
To give the rooms warmth and personality without spending much money.

The Solution:
Tortora and Crawford used their own firm's fabrics and wallpaper.
Fabric conveys the sense of softness and warmth they wanted and pattern gives them the punch and personality.

In the living room a mixed bag of furnishings is made to coordinate by being covered in the same fabric. In the dining room, a patterned paper (plus a Mexican serape) gives visual interest to the simply furnished room.

In both bedrooms, slanted walls are harmonized by covering walls and ceiling continuously in the same pattern. In one room, the slanted wall itself is the inspiration for a slanted fabric headboard. Fabric is draped on the diagonal from a square frame attached to the ceiling. The headboard lining pattern is repeated on bed bolster, upholstered chair and on the cushions of a wicker chair to provide a contrast with the simple geometric background.

In the other bedroom the bold floral pattern continues to cover a love seat and an upholstered chair so they blend into the background and avoid an overpowering additional contrast. A complimentary plain headboard is ingenious and inexpensive. It is a piece of plywood covered with foam and then wrapped in gathered black chintz.

The designers used paint cleverly.
In the dining room, Tortora and Crawford painted and spackled the floor to resemble the marble graining of the dining-table top.

In the floral bedroom, the floor, amusingly, is painted to look like old-time linoleum. With all the current interest in Art Deco and the styles of the 1930s, "linoleum" (or at least its image) has achieved a trendy chic.

The serene screen porch has a floor coated with durable outdoor deck paint.

They used some formal pieces for fun.
In the living room the Louis XVI chairs are made more informal with white paint. An 18th-century Venetian gilt console has the snooty starch taken out of it by the contrast of bunches of inexpensive wicker baskets.

In the dining room, complimentary curves coordinate fancy 19th-century gilt-decorated black chairs and Saarinen's clean classic table. Any preening pretense of formality is knocked out by the socko serape.

In the brown bedroom a formal gold-rope ottoman provides an unexpected surprise.

Sources:
All fabrics and wallpaper: QUADRILLE WALLPAPERS, INC. *Dining-room table:* KNOLL. *Rug:* ROSECORE. *Most other furnishings were at hand.*

Photographer: Richard Champion

Camping in the Country

Who: Interior concept by architect Paul Rudolph
Client—A sophisticated and adventuresome young couple—
investment banker Lee M. Elman and his graphics designer
wife, Dorothea
Where: A beautiful house in Aston Magna, home
of the Berkshires' brilliantly acclaimed Baroque music
festival, in Great Barrington, Massachusetts

Photographer: Robert Perron

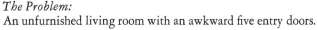

The Problem:
An unfurnished living room with an awkward five entry doors.

The Solution:
The Elmans had their friend architect Paul Rudolph for the weekend.

They must have casually asked his opinion about what to do with their living room. Rudolph realized that the first concern was the traffic patterns to and from the five doorways. To figure out where people would walk and to play a bit of a weekend game, he borrowed some light-blue swimming-pool paint, which was being used nearby for a pool-painting party, grabbed a long-handled paint roller and traced the trek from each door to all the others. Where there seemed to be open areas out of the path of traffic, he wound the stripes into circles to delineate centers for conversation.

Having fun with his traffic pattern, he dribbled some red paint in the centers of the circles to tell people to "stop," and he dribbled yellow by the doors to signal "caution"—proceed with care.

Admiring the finished effect, Rudolph and the Elmans thought the swirling circles suggested old-fashioned rural rugs—hooked or braided. Instead of wiping out the playful pattern, they daringly decided to keep it.

Now what to use for furniture? What would suit the rural imagery and the traffic tracks? "What else but tractor tires?" offered Rudolph.

Dorothea Elman made furniture of tractor tires.

She rounded up tractor tires and airplane tires of several sizes and lighted on the idea of upholstering their bulging girth in girdle fabric. A decorator neighbor, Priscilla Houston, helped her work out the details. Fabric is drawn together on strings around the tires (like the top of a duffel bag). Smaller airplane tires are bolted to the tractor tires to make backrests. Circles of clear acrylic are inserted into the empty centers to make some tires into tables.

In the sophisticated setting of Aston Magna, this rural imagery is as campy as Marie Antoinette playing shepherdess amid the splendors of Versailles.

Designers Can Enhance the Architecture of Your Home

Worn Walls Wear Fabric for Insulation and Interest

Who: Interior Designer—Kelly Amen, ASID
Client—A professional couple
Where: A badly worn, 60-year-old-house in Houston, Texas

The Problem:
1. The walls were badly worn.
2. The spaces were "woefully inadequate" in terms of insulation and acoustics.
3. The clients wanted an interesting yet relaxing environment at a reasonable price.

The Solution:
Upholstered walls and ceilings.

Kelly Amen answered all architectural problems with one clever concept. By wrapping walls and ceilings in fabric, he not only hid the worn walls; he insulated the home from noise and heat.

"You could hear pages turning from the ground-floor living room to the attic loft before we upholstered," Amen recalls. The effect on the air temperature was noticeable also—dropping some 10 degrees cooler in the master bedroom (where the ceiling was covered with suede).

At no more cost than a standard sheet-rock and paint treatment, Amen's solution avoided the need for actual architectural alterations, while providing the plus of a consistently soft and comforting interior environment.

A variety of upholstery techniques are employed in order to differentiate the rooms.

Upholsterer Thomas Goodwin used several tricks of his trade.

In a guest room (left) tucked away on the third floor attic/loft, he installed wide-waled panels of natural cotton edged with fat, cushy welts.

In a converted bedroom that was to function as a combination yoga/guest room, he stretched shirred muslin across the walls and draped it tent fashion over the ceiling.

In the dining room, he achieved a tailored yet elegant effect by box pleating an oyster moire fabric.

Within the relaxing, soft-textured, neutral-colored environment occasional hard textures and bright colors lend liveliness.

In the attic bedroom, the sisal rug, the sharp twiggy tree and exotic pillows save visitors from sinking soporiferously into the warm womb.

In the yoga/guest room, a chest suggests a contrast, as do the bright batik pillows, but the mood is still conducive to contemplation.

Photographer: Michelle Maier

Sources:
Attic/loft guest bedroom (left): *Rattan table:* CARL RENTZ. *Pillows:* CHINA SEAS, *through* VIVIAN WATSON. *Wall fabric:* RALPH LEGGETT. *Sofa table:* HENREDON. *Light fixture:* PASHA. *Sisal rug:* MELANGE. *Bedding: custom, through* HEINES.
Yoga/guest room (right): *Muslin wall fabric:* RALPH LEGGETT. *Pillows:* CHINA SEAS. *Sisal carpet:* SAXONY. *Window shades:* PASHA.

From Cold to Cozy

Who: Interior Designer—Robert Metzger
*Client—A show house to raise money for the Kips Bay
Boys Club*
*Where: A massive New York mansion, with high ceilings and
cold stone walls and floors*

The Problem:
1. The large stone space seemed cold and formidable.
2. The room was to be used as a studio apartment.

The Solution:
Massive furniture and tall trees suit the size of the space.

A large-scale sofa facing the fireplace, a big bed at one end of the room and a comfortable reading chair with a wrap-around back and an ottoman at the other end of the room balance the big space. These large upholstered pieces also soften the space.

Tall trees acknowledge the size of the ceilings, while their leafy branches cast softening shadows on the cold stone walls.

A large-scale 18th-century English secretary is an appropriate

Photographer: Jaime Ardiles-Arce

2

3

Sources:
(1) Bed, bedside table, bedside lamp: RON SEFF CREATIVE FINISHES. *Linens:* PRATESI. *Calder mobile:* ANITA KAHN FINE ARTS. *Bronze lioness, Korean tables:* GARRICK C. STEPHENSON. *Étagère, mirror on stand, Obi pillow:* KARL SPRINGER. *Ottoman:* RAY MURRAY. *All fabrics and leathers throughout:* CLARENCE HOUSE. *Draperies and shade:* JULES EDLIN. *All plants and flowers:* RENNY. *All interior painting:* ED BUCHEN.
(2) Japanese chest on chest: MATHEW SCHULTZ LTD. *Cloisonné roosters, round mirror, lucite lamp, Obi pillow:* KARL SPRINGER *Antique mirror on chest:* CHRISTIAN THEE. *Painting:* ADOLPH GOTTLIEB, *through* MARLBOROUGH GALLERY INC.
(3) Indian Dhurrie rug: DORIS LESLIE BLAU GALLERY. *Iron candlesticks:* MARVIN ALEXANDER. *Coffee table, bridal chests:* ROUNDTREE. *18th-century English secretary:* PAUL MARTINI. *Louis XV desk chair:* GARRICK C. STEPHENSON. *Bronze desk lamp:* LA VITRINE. *Painting:* LEE KRASNER, *through* MARLBOROUGH GALLERY INC. *Black chinoiserie chair:* FREDERICK VICTORIA. *Sofa, chair, ottoman:* RAY MURRAY. *Torchère:* KARL SPRINGER. *Mantel accessories:* ARNE SCHLESCH, JOSE JUAREZ GARZA.

corresponding size. A console table on the wall behind the sofa suitably serves for dining and entertaining.
Curved patterns and warm colors enliven the stark space.

The same large-scale floral pattern is used on major upholstered pieces to tie the room together. A color picked from the flowers becomes the basis of a patterned area rug defining the conversation circle. A stack of bridal chests picks up the pink flower theme. The reading corner is enlivened with a gold-on-black winding viny pattern. Even the stylized Dhurrie rug is floral in concept. The curves of nature soften the stark geometric lines of the room. The warm color of the field of the rug is repeated around the ceiling moldings, infusing even the room's heights with warmth.
Lots of accessories personalize the place.

Robert Metzger envisioned this room as an ideal environment for an incurable collector. This room almost *needs* an incurable collector to make it livable and lively.

From Dark and Dreary to Bright and Light

Who: Interior Designer—architect Benjamin Baldwin
Client—A banker who admits to "never having appreciated
forms, colors or textures before"
Where: A 1927-vintage Florida-Spanish house

Photographer: Norman McGrath

The Problem:

In Baldwin's words, the house was "extremely dark and depressing—gloomy beyond belief." The client "wanted it changed so that his family could feel happy, cheerful and bright in it. They are fond of light, brightness and color."

The Solution:

Baldwin stripped off the excessive ornament.

He removed a great deal of what he calls the "Hansel and Gretel filigree"—the black wrought-iron grillwork that covered the windows and the black iron sconces throughout the house.

He removed the 1920s Spanish Renaissance fireplace and some carvings in the wood-beamed ceiling structure.

He made the most of the light coming in the windows.

The living-room window on the entry front was heightened. The two windows flanking the fireplace became unobstructed fixed sheets of glass in flat plaster archways. To reflect light, all original windowsills were replaced with white marble sills.

Baldwin restructured the division between living room and dining room in order to leave openings in front of the windows. Originally there were side walls and a center doorway. Now there are side openings and a center H-shaped bar/credenza.

Baldwin also tore down the walls that squared off the stairwell so that light could flow through the space from the central skylight.

He lightened the dark ceiling and woodwork.

He stripped the cypress ceiling of the living room of its heavy opaque layers of paint and stained it lightly. The original wood doors and trim throughout the house were refinished to show their light natural graining.

He simplified the architecture with bold horizontal strokes.

The blue-tile hearth of the modernized fireplace in the living room is carried across the space to make a simple platform that incorporates two window seats.

The living-room balcony was redesigned as a deep white plaster panel in order to conceal air-conditioning ducts above the lowered dining-room ceiling and to house recessed and can down-lighting.

Built-in lighting reflects on white walls.

In addition to the recessed and can lighting, Baldwin designed special lighting fixtures to wash the walls and further infuse the interior with light. To complete the scheme, living-room table lights are chosen in a similarly simple shape.

Baldwin gave the floors a smooth, light look.

The floor surface from the entry hall to the study and kitchen is one continuous slick surface of tile, accented with natural wool rugs of a like light color.

Furniture is bold and simply shaped.

An antique rug wall hanging repeats and balances the shape of the entry door/window and sets the color theme of the living room. Two boldly scaled and boldly colored seating groupings are placed back to back to satisfy living needs and to stand up to the large high-ceilinged space. The sofas repeat the horizontal of the hearth and balcony; the chairs repeat the curve of the arched windows.

The bedroom echoes established themes.

A central separation backs the bed and allows a free flow of light and air to the sides. A horizontally shaped shelf recalls the living-room balcony, while arched end doors suggest the living-room windows. Lights are recessed in the ceiling or wall-mounted. The carpeted floor is smooth and light-looking.

The porch presents perky variations of the theme.

Here the floor tiles are checkerboard. With the large arched doors pouring sunshine into the space, there is no danger that the dark tiles will absorb too much light. Wicker furniture and large planters express a garden theme, while overhead fans suggest the exotic allure of Casablanca.

Photographer: Norman McGrath

Sources:
Living room: Blue tile on hearth: AMERICAN OLEAN COBALT NO. 3 installed by TILE SETTERS INC. Red lacquered round table on hearth: SIAMESE, through ART ASIA, New York. Lambskin cushions on hearth: GUCCIONE, New York. Natural Tisca wool rug: ZOGRAPHOS, New York. End tables in glass with chrome bases: HELIKON. Table lamps: NESSEN LAMPS, INC. Ashtrays: BRICKEL ASSOCIATES, WARD BENNETT DESIGN. Sofas in red glove leather: LINEA PLUS, LTD., through SORMANI, New York. Magenta chairs: TECH FURNITURE, New York; wool fabric: JACK LARSEN. Floor tile: original "CUBAN" glazed tile. Wall light fixtures: HARRY GITLIN from design by BENJAMIN BALDWIN; shades: IRENE LAMPSHADES, New York, fabric: BORIS KROLL. Wall hanging: ANTIQUE TUNISIAN RUG from THE PILLOWRY, New York. Ceiling track lighting: LIGHTOLIER. Recessed ceiling light fixtures: LIGHTOLIER.

Hall: Carpet: EDWARD FIELDS. Hat rack: STENDIG. Table with laminated Indian print: KARL SPRINGER. Wood bowl: SIAMESE through ART ASIA. Paper lantern: BONNIERS.
Bedroom: Fabric for curtains, bedcover, cushions: BOUSSAC. Chaise: HARVEY PROBBER. Coffee table: KNOLL. Side chair in linen: BRUNO MATHSSON from SCANDINAVIAN DESIGN. Bedside lights: HARRY GITLIN.
Dining room: Dining table in white marble with stainless-steel base: BRUETON. Chairs: BRICKEL ASSOCIATES, WARD BENNETT design, vinyl seat fabric: J. H. THORP. Red formica liquor tray: BENJAMIN BALDWIN design, custom-made. Rug: ZOGRAPHOS.
Porch: Planters: ARTEC through ROBERT BENJAMIN; Wicker chairs: BIELECKY; fabric: BORIS KROLL. Ottomans: BIELECKY; fabric: BOUSSAC. Ceiling fans: ROBBINS & MEYERS, Memphis, Tenn. Wire tables: KNOLL. Dining table: BENJAMIN BALDWIN design in white formica with wood edges. Dining chairs: McGUIRE; printed fabric: BOUSSAC; blue fabric: BORIS KROLL.
General contractor: ERSKINE EARNEST, Miami. Associated landscape architect: ALLEN FERNANDEZ, Miami. Electrical: CRAWFORD ELECTRIC CO. Cabinet work: ROLU WOODCRAFTERS. Custom furniture: WILLIAM PETTIT, Sarasota. Curtains, bedcovers: NORMAN SEIDLER INC., Miami.

DESIGNERS CAN ENHANCE ARCHITECTURE

Cotton Warehouse Becomes Restoration Residence

Where: The oldest cotton warehouse on the eastern seaboard. Built in 1816 when cotton was king in the South, the William Taylor Warehouse on the banks of the Savannah River has survived the years (and General Sherman). When the Historic Savannah Foundation was organized in 1955, preserving the waterfront, where the city started, was one of its primary objectives.

Who: Dr. and Mrs. C. Lamont Osteen saw the potential of a restoration residence. Mrs. Osteen, who is an artist, says she was originally attracted to the warehouse because "it was the earliest one," and (unlike the others) "it had a wonderful pitched roof" for her studio skylight. Mrs. Osteen, formerly a decorator at Hutzler's in Baltimore, worked closely with Savannah architect Juan Bertotto.

The Problem:
1. To renovate the top two floors to make them work as a home.
2. To take advantage of the building's unique architectural assets.

The Solution:
The architect opened the interior to light from the skylighted studio.

He carved a stairwell out of the heart of the house to allow light to flow through. At the bottom of the sloping skylight he removed the flooring so that light could shine through the exposed floor joists to the living/dining room below.

To separate the kitchen and the library from the living/dining area, he put them behind curved 7-foot-high partitions. The partitions define the areas without stopping the high horizontal flow of light and air.

The beams of the sloping skylight wall inspired the ceiling of the living/dining room.

Diagonally laid pine strips form a ceiling in the living/dining area that suggests a similarity with the wall upstairs.

An original wooden elevator wheel is an influence.

A 13-foot-diameter elevator wheel that was originally used to hoist bales of cotton up and down the five stories of the warehouse is suspended at the top of the stairwell. Its shape inspires a circular brick fireplace set in the center of the loft living area and the center-pivoting doorways of the bedrooms to its sides.

Textures and colors are chosen to suit the architecture.

Made of ballast stone, Savannah gray brick and heart pine, the rich textures and colors of the warehouse structure are enhanced by off-white walls, furniture of natural materials and rich color accents selected by Mrs. Osteen. Some of her own paintings hang on the walls.

Sources:
Breuer chairs: STENDIG. *Lighting:* LIGHTOLIER. *Arc lamp:* LIGHTING ASSOCIATES. *Paint (Savannah Spectrum):* MARTIN SENOUR. *Cabinet-work:* WILMINGTON CABINETS *(Savannah).* *Fabricator of fireplace:* DELTA METALS *(Savannah).*

Designers Can Blend the Old and the New

Photographer: Taylor Lewis

Enlightening the Past

Who: Interior Designer—Allan D. Ivie III of J. Frank Jones/
Allan Denny Ivie Associates, Inc.
Client—The wife of the Governor of Virginia at the time,
Mrs. Mills E. Godwin, Jr.
Where: The historic Governor's Mansion in Richmond, Virginia,
originally designed in 1811 by the Boston architect
Alexander Parris

The Problem:

To perk up the tired-looking and dark ballroom. The room had to stand up to heavy use for large and small public functions, and it had to be pleasant for private living for this and subsequent Governors' families.

The Solution:

The designer made the most of the past.

By respecting the Federal architecture and the original 18th-century English-style furnishings and continuing that tradition, the designer defined an environment that would inspire the public as well as please a series of successful Governors.

For safety's sake, he placed irreplaceable antiques out of harm's way at the ends of the room. To harmonize with the antiques and to stand up to constant use, he specified sturdy reproductions of 18th-century English styles for the rest of the room.

Opposite the fireplaces in both wings, camel-back Chippendale sofas define centers for conversation. By the fireplaces, two 18th-century fan-back chairs in the south wing and a reproduction wing chair in the north provide other anchors for conversational groups. All other 18th-century-style seating is light and easily moved—changed and rearranged for different social gatherings.

Light colors and shiny textures simulate sunlight.

Designer Ivie wanted the ballroom to radiate light instead of devour it. A white, ivory and gold silk and linen brocatelle fabric is the source of his scheme. He framed the windows in it; covered the camel-back sofas and also the wing chair. He took the ivory tone of the background and painted the walls and ceilings that soft sunshine color. He picked up the gold in drapery trim and tassels and in gilt frames for mirrors over the mantels and portraits of prominent Virginians. He spilled gold sunlight all over the floor in two wool cut-pile carpets and spread the shine in a satin upholstery for Hepplewhite wheel-back armchairs and a two-back Chippendale settee. The mirrors and the crystal chandeliers further reflect and refract the light.

The designer has devised a happy way to live today while respecting and preserving the past.

Sources:
Drapery fabric and fringe: SCALAMANDRE. *Custom carpets:* EDWARD MOLINA DESIGNS. *Chippendale camel-back sofas:* JOSEPH GIANOLA; *fabric:* SCALAMANDRE. *Sheraton-style open armchairs:* KAPLAN; *fabric:* BRUNSCHWIG & FILS. *Hepplewhite wheel-back armchairs:* SMITH AND WATSON; *fabric:* BRUNSCHWIG & FILS. *Antique 18th-century fan-back chair fabric:* CLARENCE HOUSE. *Chippendale two-back settee:* JOHN SCALIA-SCHMIEG AND KOTZIAN; *fabric:* BRUNSCHWIG & FILS. *Wing chair:* KITTINGER; *fabric:* SCALAMANDRE.

In the Old French Fashion

Who: Interior Designer—Joseph John Potter
Client—The Joseph B. Lantermans
Where: The library of an apartment in one of the best-built
pre-1930 cooperatives on Chicago's Lake Shore Drive

The Problem:
To restore the fine Louis XV architectural detailing that had been originally installed by architect David Adler and to complete the furnishing of the room.

The Solution:
Paneling, flooring and fireplace were restored to original brightness.

The library features finely carved Louis XV oak paneling, thought to have been imported from a French chateau. Designer Potter discovered the original blueprints and restored the wood to its initial honey tone. The fine antique rose marble fireplace and the parquet floor were cleaned.

Curved styles were chosen for their compatibility with Louis XV.

The dominant shape of the Louis XV style is curved. Designer Potter kept to consistent curves. He chose a sofa and armchair with

Photographer: Orlando Cabanban

curved arm detailing. He selected an open armchair in an actual Louis XV style. He used curved French occasional tables, both antique and reproduction. He modeled draperies with double swag valances after an elaborate French treatment. He even specified scalloped bottoms for the window shades.

Potter varies the characteristics traditional to Louis XV in order to suit the situation.

In the time of Louis XV there was a fashion for things Chinese and even Indian. Potter picked up on the Eastern interest with a Persian Tabriz carpet. Its motifs are curved, and its colors convey a warm richness compatible with the wood paneling and rose marble fireplace.

The carpet colors are deep blue, red and gray. Instead of using the pale pastels traditional to the Louis XV style, Potter chose a scheme inspired by the deep colors of the carpet. The sofa and club chair have a blue upholstery with a dark-red square dot pattern. The draperies, window shades and occasional chair are a printed cotton Persian pattern with boldly scaled blue flowers and leaves on a red ground.

The scale of the pattern works well with the large size of the sofa and club chair. The large sizes and the bold colors are a departure from the traditional Louis XV style but are completely compatible with comfort and the climate of Chicago.

Sources:
Sofa: LAKESIDE UPHOLSTERY COMPANY; *upholstery:* BORIS KROLL. *Occasional tables (antique and reproduction):* RICHARD NORTON *(Chicago). Coffee table in front of sofa:* YALE R. BURGE. *Mini chest at end of sofa:* MELDAN *(Chicago). Drapery fabric:* PATTERSON-PIAZZA, INC. *Chinese lamp rewiring and moleskin sconce shades:* LAN I. LEVIN *(Chicago).*

Entertaining Preferences

Who: Architect—John T. McMahon
Interior Designer—Jova/Daniels/Busby
Client—A family epitomizing Southern hospitality
by entertaining often
Where: A five-bedroom home in Atlanta, Georgia

The Problem:
1. To create an environment for entertaining.
2. To blend a new home with old furnishings.

The Solution:
To encourage entertaining, the architect separated quiet areas from noisy ones.

The house was planned with the living room, two studies and the master bedroom at one end, the foyer and dining room in the center and the children's rooms, playroom and guest room on the other end.

To combine the old and the new, the designers emphasized the differences between them.

The dynamic of the design is contrast—contrast between stark, staring modern and soft, warm old.

The lines of the modern home are sharp and clean. The designers emphasized this crisp geometric character in the living room with bands of black on the off-white walls. They brought the modern message to the furniture with two white rectangles for sofas and two dark rectangles on cold chrome for benches.

Against this stark scene they played off the romance of the old. They gave everything old a soft texture and a rich color. A Chinese rug in warm burgundy and blues centers the scene. An antique armchair is upholstered in plain purple but backed in patterned velvet. Curvy Louis XV bergère chairs are upholstered in a warm leather look. An ornate mirror and console provide additional antique éclat.

The ottoman is the only compromise with contrast. It is modern, warmly colored and softly shaped. It helps to harmonize the dramatically diverse scheme.

The living room is the central statement; other rooms are variations of the theme.

In the master bedroom color contrasts are minimized in the interest of serenity, but the hard crisp lines of the architecture contrast with the enveloping softness of the furniture. A contemporary lounge chair and ottoman are upholstered in cut velvet. The French Provincial-style bed is swathed in fur. Detailed decorative interest is provided by a pierced ceramic garden table and a soft Spanish painting.

The playroom is completely modern. The idea of a graphic wall treatment, expressed in the living room, becomes more pointed here. A straight-lined sofa and bench repeat the colors and multi-directional theme of the walls. A rush-seated chair and bright green and red seats and pillows provide contrast within the slick-surfaced, neutral-colored modern mood. Of course, a billiard table and a half-dozen pinball machines are the real focus of fun.

Sources:
Living room: Draperies, fabric: ISABEL SCOTT; *fabricator:* DAVIS-NEAL, INC. *Sofas:* DIRECTIONAL; *fabric:* JACK LENOR LARSEN. *Bergères:* STEPHEN MALLORY. *Antique armchair:* THE BROWNSTONE; *fabric:* CLARENCE HOUSE *and* JACK LENOR LARSEN. *Benches and ottoman:* HELIKON; *fabric:* JACK LENOR LARSEN. *Coffee table:* JOSEPH LOMBARDO, INC. *End tables:* EPPINGER. *Side table:* THE WRECKING BAR. *Plants:* PLANT HOUSE.
Master bedroom: Lounge chair and ottoman: HARVEY PROBBER; *fabric:* CLARENCE HOUSE. *Bed throw:* TROPHY HIDES. *Garden table:* EDITH HILLS. *Drapery, fabric:* THAIBOK *from* JACK LENOR LARSEN; *fabricator:* DAVIS-NEAL, INC.
Playroom: Vinyl asbestos floor tile: KENTILE. *Sisal area rug:* ALISON T. SEYMOUR. *Lounge and side chairs:* ATELIER INTERNATIONAL. *Stack tables:* BEYLERIAN. *Game table:* HERMAN MILLER. *Plants:* PLANT HOUSE.

Photographer: Claude May

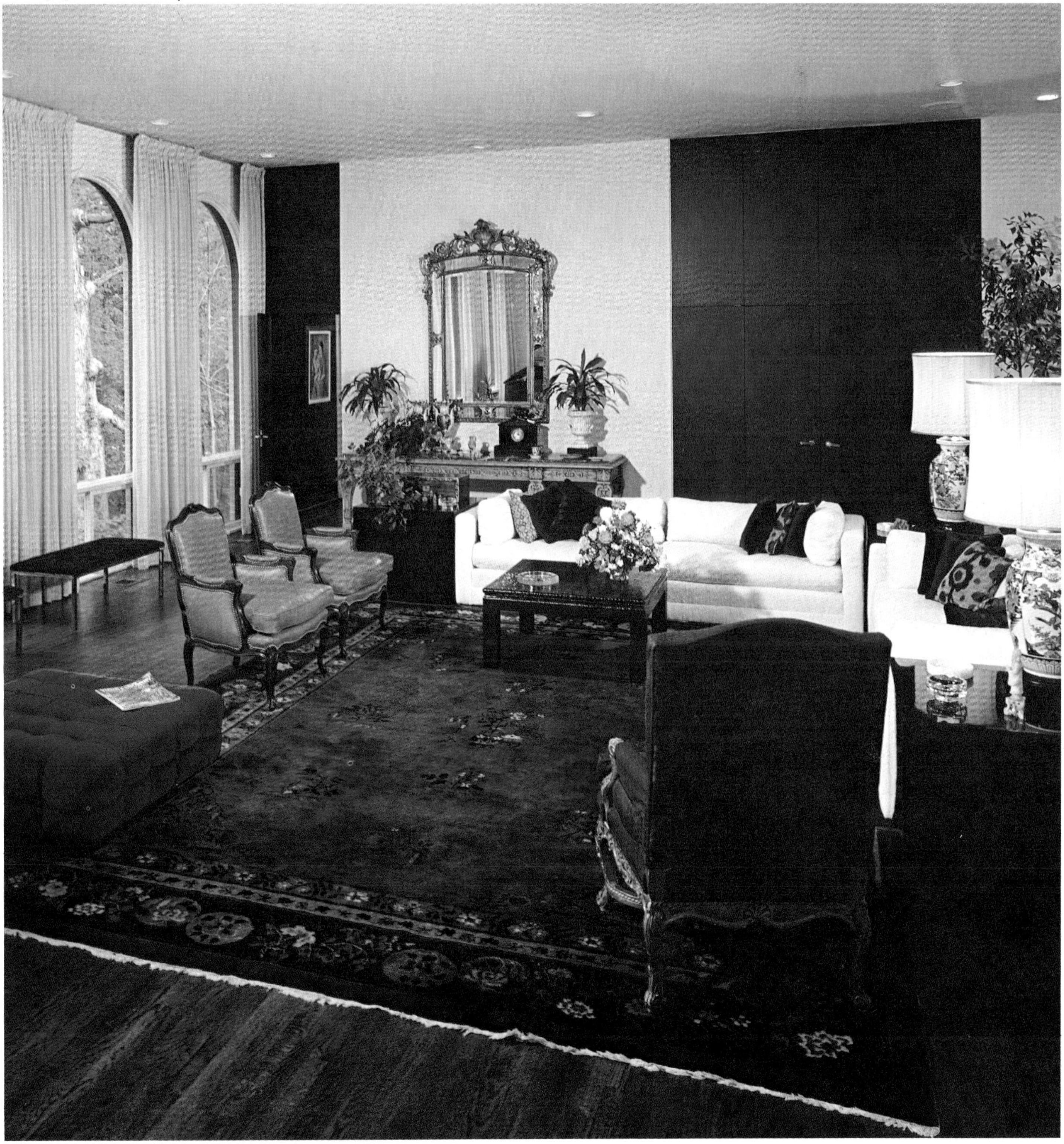

A New Lease on Life

Who: Interior Designer—Mrs. Russell Davenport in association with John Drews and J. Neil Stevens of McMillen, Inc. Client—A peripatetic couple with grown children who wanted to move from their authentic 18th-century French style home to a modern pied à terre in New York City Where: They found what they wanted—"a small apartment conveniently located in a well-operated building"—in a substantial old building overlooking Central Park

Photographer: Louis Reens

Sources:
General contractor: WILLIAM CRAWFORD. *Wallcoverings:* WOLF-GORDON. *Painting and wallcovering installation:* NORTHERN PAINT-ING & DECORATION, INC.
Dining room: Chair upholstery: JOSEPH JACOBS. *Table designed by* POILLERAT *for* McMILLEN.
Living room: Banquette fabric: ISABEL SCOTT. *Directoire tub chair upholstery:* JOSEPH JACOBS. *Custom-design coffee table:* J. PAUL JONES. *Brass lounge chairs:* DOMAS; *upholstery:* BRUNSCHWIG & FILS. *Roman shade fabric:* & VICE VERSA. *Plant:* JEAN JACQUES BLOOS. *Basket:* DAVID BARRETT.

The Problem:
1. The couple had had enough of 18th-century French authenticity; they wanted a modern scheme, but they still wanted to use many of their fine museum-quality antiques.
2. Since they travel a lot, they wanted the apartment to be easy to maintain.
3. Even though the apartment they chose has only one bedroom, they wanted a guest room to accommodate their grown children when they visit.

The Solution:
To make a modern mood, the designers made the apartment seem spacious.

The designers made architectural adaptations to make the space seem fluid. They closed off the bathroom door facing the visitor at the entry. They rounded the dining room wall to the right of the entry. They opened up the sides of the wall between the adjacent living room and the study so that the two small rooms would seem like one. Furthering the illusion, the designers built in bookcases along the east walls of both rooms and treated the windows on the west walls the same way.

To stretch the space and make it flow, they covered the floors in this entertaining area in a continuous expanse of slick, pale travertine. To keep the background unbroken and serenely simple, they chose a mottled light-tan vinyl wallcovering to match the tone and texture of the travertine.

To emphasize the extension of space to the outdoors, the designers replaced the old small-paned windows with single sheets of glass that allow an unobstructed view of Central Park.
They incorporated modern machinery for convenience.

They ran air-conditioning ducts from a window unit—located in a closet of the dressing room—to the perimeters of the living room and bedroom. To accommodate the ducts, the designers lowered the ceiling in the dressing room and dining room and around the perimeters of the bedroom, living room and study. The lowered ceiling allowed the incorporation of inset down-lights and a smashing semicircular cove wall-wash in the dining room.

The lighting is controlled from a theaterlike bank of switches kept in a closet off the dining area. There are remote dimmers and preset on-off controls. Very sophisticated.

In the bedroom, a motorized bed eliminates the need for a headboard. Lights and sound are controlled from a custom-designed bedside console.
The designers built in and bought modern furnishings.

To brighten and excite the time-worn patina of the couple's museum-quality antiques, the designers bought and built slick modern styles. In the living room a built-in sofa banquette and contemporary French armchairs with brass frames set off the Directoire tub chairs in cinnamon suede.

In the dining room the chairs are fine Louis XVI antiques. The slick custom-designed dining table was created to be complimentary.

In the bedroom a marquetry-and-ormolu Regence commode is flanked by deep brown plastic chairs.
The study was designed to double as a guest room.

The central partition-divider between the living room and study incorporates sliding doors that can be closed to create a place of privacy. The sofa in the study is a convertible bed. The console facing the sofa incorporates storage space as well as TV, hi-fi and records.
Materials are easy to maintain.

The travertine floors are easy to clean, and so, certainly, are the vinyl walls. Amazingly, the curved cove in the dining area that looks like finely finished lacquer is also vinyl—in a deep, rich burgundy color.

Pared to Perfection

Who: Interior Designer—Ron Oates, formerly of San Francisco,
now of the New York design firm Circanow Ltd.
Where: The designer's previous apartment in a pretty pastel
building on San Francisco's Nob Hill

The Problem:

The apartment had a gracious amount of space and interesting decorative detail, but the original architecture was buried under layers of damask wallpaper and unsightly thicknesses of paint.

The Solution:

Oates stripped the place clean.

He removed the wallpaper and stripped down the paint to reveal the apartment's basic architectural assets. The airy apartment has handsome plank wood floors, streamlined moldings, curlicued capitals atop fluted columns and a cozy inglenook by the fire with built-in banquettes for seating and a beveled mirror over the mantel.

Through color Oates emphasized the spaciousness of the living area and the coziness of the nook.

In the living area, walls and windows are unified by being a single stretch of white. A white area rug flows the floor together with the walls to complete an air of openness.

In the fireplace nook, walls are warm brown to contribute to the sense of a cozy enclosure.

New furnishings are harmonized with old architecture through similarity of shape.

A slick modular sofa system is arranged to repeat the rectangular shape of the room. Its dark-brown color underlines the impact.

To repeat the curves of the columns, Oates stood simple, industrial Sono tubes in the corner. (They also served to store his out-of-season clothes.) To reiterate the fluting of the columns, designer Oates chose a dining table with a ribbed base.

All furnishings are pure, sleek and simple.

To harmonize with the simple shapes of the sofa and Sono tubes, Oates chose other furnishings of unadorned forms. The coffee table is a cube; the dining-table top, a trapezoid. The dining chairs are Breuer's curved classic. Lighting and accessories are minimal, crisp and clean. "I hate clutter," admits Oates.

An artwork coordinates the themes of the scheme.

A wall-hung artwork of geometric forms and neutral colors ties together the scheme and provides a focal point for the living room. The apartment's stunning simplicity sets off its architectural assets.

Sources:
Fireplace inglenook: Table: KNOLL INTERNATIONAL. *Pillows:* KNEEDLER-FAUCHERE. *Vases:* VENINI, KNOLL INTERNATIONAL.
Living room: Seating: MIREMONT-FALK. *Lighting:* LUXO, AXIOM DESIGNS. *Window treatment:* WARREN'S OF CALIFORNIA. *Artwork:* VICTO OTTANELLI, *through* ALLRICH GALLERY. *Accessories:* AXIOM DESIGNS. *Plants:* PACIFIC NURSERIES.
Dining area: Dining table: KNOLL INTERNATIONAL. *Chairs:* THE CHAIR STORE. *Framed poster:* SOURCE GALLERY. *Lighting:* KOVAKS/DESIGN MART S.R.

Photographer: Bob Van Noy

A Surprising Synthesis

Who: Architect—Hardy Holzman Pfeiffer Associates
Project Architect—Peter Wilson
Client—The client's children now had families of their own,
and so she wanted a smaller, more compact, more
convenient house than the one she had.
Where: Ardsley, New York

Photographer: Norman McGrath

The Problem:

1. The client wanted a new house built for her. She thought she might like a contemporary style. "I would like a house to suit me as I am now," she explained to architect Hugh Hardy.
2. She expected to use her antique furniture in her new home. "The thought that if she built a contemporary house she must throw off her whole past and rush off to Bloomingdale's and surround herself with chromium lamps and plush rugs didn't cross her mind for a minute," reports Hardy.

The Solution:

The home achieves its design impact through the contrast between contemporary architecture and traditional furnishings.

Architect Hardy emphasizes, "The relationship between things can be a design as much as the spaces themselves. When you think that we take real car wrecks and hang them on the walls of art galleries, and that the act of hanging them on the wall out of context creates a design, then that act of design can be equally valid in a house." Taking things out of their normal context can create fresh perspectives. Think of what Andy Warhol achieved by taking the Campbell soup can off the kitchen shelf!

The architecture offers a variety of spatial experiences.

The house is arranged in an A-shape plan. One enters just before the crossbar of the A. A long hall going from one side of the house to the other *is* the crossbar of the A. From the hall, one steps up a level to the centered dining room and its flanking kitchen and study. From this middle level one walks up some more stairs to the living room.

The ceilings of the dining room and living room open to a two-story height. The shape is described by a green-painted steel structure that forms a rotated square (see picture, left).

This variety of flooring levels and ceiling levels lends excitement to the scheme.

Red head-height cabinets separate areas within the wall-less living area.

The lack of walls allows space to flow up the three levels and up to the two-story ceiling. The architects didn't want to block views of the vistas.

While the crimson color is complimentary to the wood tones of the client's many mahogany antiques, it puts the emphasis on the background rather than on the foreground furnishings.

Emphasis is on the background rather than the foreground.

Following the emphasis on the background, rich rugs ornament the floor. A decorative floral wallpaper covers the walls of the crossbar hallway.

The fine furnishings, mostly 18th- and 19th-century English and American pieces collected over the past 35 to 40 years, are underplayed. Actually, the seeming underplay is not. The strong background silhouettes the lovely lines of the antiques. White or light furnishings are set off by the bright-red contrasting color, and the rich and ornamental textures of the furnishings gain piquancy in opposition to the plain structural surfaces.

PART THREE
How to Work with an Interior Designer

Finding the Look You Like

1. What look would you like in your home? It depends on how you and the other members of your household feel. Is home anyplace you hang your hat? Then you had better be able to move it easily. Is it where your heart is? Then it should be the place where you keep the things (and people) you love. Is it your castle? It should make you feel like a king, and protect you from the outside world. *The look should fit your dreams.*

2. What does it take to make *you* feel happy and relaxed? What do you enjoy? What do you daydream about? As an experiment, close your eyes and think happy thoughts. What images come before your mind? Where are you? What are you doing? A designer might be able to suggest the happy thoughts of your fantasies in the design of your home. For example, if you are dreaming of a vacation in a certain place, a designer might use the colors of that landscape and the crafts of that place to suggest its atmosphere in your home. *The look should fit your realities.*

Your home should deal with the realities of your life—the ages and stages of the people living with you, the characteristics of the climate, the pros and cons of the architecture, the furniture you have and want to use, and the money you want to spend.

Children and pets suggest the selection of durable and stain-proof materials. A hot climate suggests cool colors and slick textures. A cold climate suggests the opposite—hot colors and thick warm textures. The architectures suggests styles of similar formality—rustic furniture for a log cabin, fancy furniture for a polished posh home. The furniture you have will guide the selection of additional furniture. The amount of money you want to spend will determine where best to invest. Designers are excellent advisers on fitting furnishings to your realities. However, they perform best if given an accurate picture of those realities. Thinking realistically about your needs will not only help you determine "the look you like," but the look that *will work* well for you.

Where can you look for inspiration?

1. *You can look through magazines, newspapers and books.*
Cut out the pictures of the products and rooms that you like. A designer can help you adapt the ideas you like to your own home. (You also might cut out pictures of things that you hate. That will tell your designer what to avoid!) A real room often ought to be more mellow than the picture. Publicity pictures and ads are usually overemphasized to promote a product. Even a room that actual people live in may be temporarily unlivable in order to dramatize it for photography.

2. *You can look at model rooms.* Pick-up brochures
Model rooms are marvelous for showing new fashion trends and suggesting ways of pulling the parts of a room together. However, some are sensational just to bring traffic to the furniture floor. The more realistic ones are still designed to promote something. Those in stores are pushing the sale of merchandise. Those in designer showhouses are showing off designers' talents in order to raise

money for charity. Those in model homes and apartments are designed to sell the real estate. Once you discount the sales pitch, you can pick up a lot of valid ideas.
If you like traditional styles, go to museums and historic restorations. Familiarize yourself with the real thing. Then you will know how to judge quality.
The role of friends and family.
The influence of outside friends and family on your choice of furnishings may be a good one or a bad one. The thing to remember is that *you must please yourself and the other members of your household.* A professional interior designer is probably more of an expert than your mother-in-law.

Finding the Right Designer for You

The important thing to remember when shopping for a designer is that *you are the boss.* It's your money as well as your home. Since it's you being charged, *you are in charge.*

How and where can you find a designer?

1. *You might find a designer through a friend's recommendation.*
You might have been impressed by the designer's work in the home of a friend, neighbor, or relative and want to see what he could do for you.

2. *You might be turned on by the model rooms in a department store.*
Usually you can buy anything in a model room except the services of its designer. The person who does the model room generally does not work with customers on residential design. This does not mean you cannot have a room just like the model room. It just means that you usually have to go to the store's design studio to get it.

3. *You might go directly to the design studio of a store you trust.*
When you go to the interior design department of a retail store, the person at the desk will assign you a designer to interview unless you ask for one specifically. If you and this designer don't get along, ask to interview another. This might cause a slightly awkward moment, but no matter; you must please yourself.

4. *You might love a room in a designer showhouse.*
Designers use showhouses to publicize their talents as well as to raise money for charity. Since they do the rooms at their own expense, they usually exhibit their own aesthetic preferences. If you want something like what you see, the designer would be delighted to hear of your interest.

5. *You might find a designer through a publication.*
You might see a designer's work published in your local newspaper, in magazines or books. If you like his look and want it for your own, get in touch with his office.
Some designers are hired especially for their "signature." They adapt their look to their client's needs, but still they have certain things they like to do. For example, Billy Baldwin has the little armless pillow chair which he puts in every job. Angelo Donghia always uses the overstuffed fat plump chair and usually a lot of gray

flannel. Mario Buatta always has flowers and prints and lots of little pictures hanging from bows.

Other designers are hired because they don't have a signature look. They can satisfy their clients' needs without leaving a sign that they were there—nothing visible except a subtle sense of harmony and beauty.

You might get a lead from the ASID.

When looking for a designer you might call the local chapter of the American Society of Interior Designers. Each ASID chapter has a referral service. In order not to show preference, the chapter will give you three or four names of designers to interview.

How to interview a designer

The next step after locating a designer is to interview him. What can you hope to accomplish in this initial interview? Basically, a mutual understanding. Honesty on the part of both parties is absolutely essential. It is the only foundation for a good relationship.

Outline the job to be done.

A good designer will ask you questions to elicit the kind of information he needs to know. First, he will want you to outline the scope of the job—whether you want to do over the whole home, just the living room, or whatever.

Tell the designer the look you'd like. What are your dreams? You might show him pictures of things you like that you've cut out of magazines. What are your realities? Describe your home. If you are in the designer's office, you might show the designer a floor plan. You might arrange with him to have a second interview at your home where you can show him your problems and the furnishings you want to use. (For an interview at your home, a designer might ask to be reimbursed for his time and traveling expenses.)

If you are in a rush to get the design job completed, be sure to tell the designer that fact. It means that he should limit himself to selecting merchandise readily available for quick delivery.

Tell the designer honestly what you have budgeted to spend.

Sometimes the question of cost raises a problem because most of us aren't used to the prices of home furnishings. We are much more familiar with the cost of clothes or coffee because we buy these items more often. Before you talk to a designer, browse around the furniture floor of a department store looking at the price tags. This will be helpful to you in setting realistic objectives.

Tell the designer truthfully what you can plan to spend. It's a designer's first duty to use your money wisely and if you take him into your confidence he can save you a good deal. Also, if he knows the truth, he can focus on the real challenge before him and not waste his time (and your money) on things that won't suit you.

Although some designers won't take jobs below a certain amount, many designers prefer low-budget jobs to ones where the sky is the limit. A low budget challenges their ingenuity, and flexes their talent. However, if what you hope to accomplish is impossible on your budget, the designer should tell you immediately. He might suggest creating a master plan which would allow you to make purchases over a five-year period. He might suggest tackling the design job room by room. He might suggest offering you many money-wise ideas in an hour's consultation. He also might suggest that you spend more than you had planned in order to achieve the effect you would like. You can always say no. *You are in control of the amount of money spent.* If you are not the person in your household signing the checks, bring this person to the interview. He should have the right of approval.

The designer should inspire you with confidence.

First of all, he must convey the feeling that he is interested in knowing you and your needs. Otherwise, how could he possibly create an interior that expresses your personality? If you feel strongly about having a certain style, you might ask the designer directly if he feels comfortable working with that style. If the designer finds what you want to be beyond his capabilities or competence, he should say so immediately and back out of the job.

Some designers have a signature look. Others can adapt themselves totally to their clients' preferences. Which type are you interviewing? Which type would you prefer? To get a feeling for the designer's own aesthetic preferences, you might ask to see examples of his work. If you interview a designer in his studio, you might see indications of his preferences. A designer might volunteer to show you photographs or slides of his work. However, some particularly adaptable designers don't like to show pictures of their work. They don't want you to assume that what they did for another client is what they would do for you. They don't want to inhibit your imagination or misrepresent their versatility.

After establishing the designer's interest in you, and his sense of style, you want to be assured of his technical ability. What is the designer's educational background and experience? The American Society of Interior Designers (ASID) has established high qualification standards for its members. The Interior Design Society (IDS) which operates in specific stores has developed educational courses and training for its members. If the designer you are interviewing is a member of either association, you can be more assured of his professional quality.

What can the designer do for you? The designer should honestly define the scope of his services. He should explain what he can, and what he cannot do for you. He might tell you that he could give you an hour's consultation or execute a complete scheme right down to the last little accessory.

Do not expect a designer to give you answers to your own design problems during the initial interview unless he is charging you a consultant's fee. Designers must be wary of people who pick their brains without engaging their services.

The designer must explain his financial methods.

Whatever this designer's financial methods, you need to know them. The more you know now, the freer you'll be from frustration later. If the designer you're interviewing seems strangely secretive about his methods of operation, go look for another designer. You have the right to know in advance how you will be charged.

Designers have many different ways of charging, and they may adjust their methods to suit the circumstances of the job. Basically, they have two choices: They may charge a fee for their time and services or they may make their money by marking up the price of merchandise. The designer and client can discuss which way or combination of ways is most suitable. Before beginning work, most designers require a deposit or retainer.

Fee Basis

Many designers today work on a fee basis. The designer's fee pays for his time and talent, his drawings, his presentations. The designer offers his client merchandise at the price he pays for it, but adds a carrying charge for his overhead and expenses—the cost of his phone calls, ordering, billing, following up, and servicing the job. A designer's fee should be commensurate with his ability.

The designer might ask for a flat fee for the job, but add a time clause to the contract, saying something like . . . if the job isn't done by such and such a date, I will charge for additional time at an hourly rate or a daily rate. If the client has caused delays, after a certain point a designer can't afford to spend more time unless he is compensated.

A designer might charge a fee on the basis of the time he spends. This allows you to engage a designer for a short while, and then call on him again later when you feel like it. In addition to time, fees are sometimes based on the square footage of the job or on a percentage of the budget.

A designer on a fee basis might submit a monthly bill. Pay it in thirty days and everybody is happy. This avoids the client getting walloped at the end, and saves the designer from waiting too long for his money.

Mark-up Basis

Many designers act as retailers. They buy wholesale and sell retail, just like a store. The designer may actually have a shop or work for a store, but not necessarily. Store-affiliated designers have an interest in moving the merchandise of their store. They may have a quota to fill, or a commission to earn. To your advantage, many stores absorb the cost of design services if you buy a certain amount of merchandise. Many independent designers prefer to work on a mark-up basis because it seems awkward to charge their clients/friends for their time.

Making an agreement

When the designer understands what you need and what you will pay and you understand what he will do for you and what he will charge, and you still like and trust each other, by all means, come to an agreement and get to work!

If you want to proceed cautiously with a designer who seems promising, you might arrange to pay him a consultant's fee for a second interview. He could come back to you with a floor plan, some sample swatches, some ideas. If you like his ideas and want him to execute his plans, you can make arrangements to proceed with the job. If you don't like his ideas, you can part company.

If you're not sure you like the designer you've interviewed, thank him politely, tell him you'll be in touch with him later, and go interview another designer. You comparative-shop for cars and coffee, why not for a designer?

Working with a Designer

There are three stages to a design job: the conception, the execution, and the installation.

The conception

After conversing with you about your needs, dreams, and design problems, the designer must go off and conceive a scheme that works on a practical and on an aesthetic level. His solution must combine the look you like with the right performance and price.

The designer must draw on all his expertise in order to orchestrate sizes, shapes, colors, textures and lighting to express your personality and satisfy your needs.

The designer might sketch out a preliminary floor plan and put together a color scheme complete with fabric and paint samples and come back to you to test out his ideas. He might show you photographs and/or sketches of furniture, drapery treatments, carpeting, and other elements.

Often a designer will present you with ideas that seem strange and unusual at first. This is not surprising. You are hiring him for his imagination, knowledge of products and awareness of fashion. He may have selected merchandise from designer showrooms, merchandise you've never seen before. He may want to have something special custom-made for you. He may want to up-date your image.

A designer will give you time to digest his ideas. He should do his level-best to explain to you why he has chosen what he has, why he thinks it would be right for you. He might take you to the designer showrooms and *show* you what he has in mind.

Your reactions will help the designer refine a scheme which is really right for you.

If you take an especially long time to decide that you like something, the item, unfortunately, may no longer be in stock when you want it. You and your designer will have to substitute.

The execution

When you and your designer are settled on what you will do in your home, the shopping, specifying and ordering can begin.

Your designer might have shown you pictures of three chairs, all of which would be appropriate for your living room. In order to decide which one you will buy, the designer might take you to the designer showrooms to sit in the chairs, touch them, and look them over. Together you might weigh the price, looks, and performance benefits of each and come to a final decision.

In order to purchase merchandise, a designer naturally needs money. He might ask you for all of it in advance, or half of it in advance and the rest upon delivery. The manufacturers that the designer deals with require money up front, even though delivery may take a long time. This is a fact of life. Most designers can't afford to sink all their own funds into ordering merchandise for you, so they must ask you for the money. They also must be responsible for charging you sales tax when applicable, or else the government will come after them!

Some sources will allow you to pay them directly, but most designer sources will not accept a check directly from you. The designer has to place the purchase order and pay with *his* check. This way the manufacturer has fewer credit references to check and feels secure dealing only with professionals.

Many designers are willing to carbon you with copies of their bills and purchase orders, if that is your agreement.

Part of the designer's job is to handle subcontractors—painters, wallpaper hangers, cabinetmakers, etc. (He might charge extra for this supervisory time.) Because a designer uses the services of these people often, he knows who is good and who offers the best value for the money. He knows how to speak their language and how to instruct them. Often he will make working drawings for them to execute. A designer can handle any problems or misunderstandings that come up between you and the subcontractor. The subcontractor will want to please the designer—his repeat business will come up sooner than yours.

A designer might also have secret sources for antiques, a man who can fix your favorite chair; he might know all sorts of people who can help make your home what you would wish. The designer might have collected special treasures in recent travels abroad; he might have friends in galleries and garrets. Part of his expertise is to know where and how to find what you want.

The installation

A good designer makes himself responsible for everything connected with your job. If the sofa arrives in the wrong color, or the draperies are too short, it is the designer's job to rectify the mistake with the supplier. For your own peace of mind, you might have this understanding written into a letter of agreement.

The only thing you can't blame your designer for is late deliveries. He can't do anything about them. A good designer will paint the bleakest possible picture in the initial interview. If you are especially eager to have your home completed quickly, you must limit yourself to ordering only merchandise that is warehoused, ready for delivery. Many custom-made items take longer, and often manufacturers misrepresent to your designer just how much longer it will be. Late deliveries are as frustrating to your designer as they are to you. It is difficult for him to take on new work until your job is completed to your satisfaction. He wants to see your smile as he puts the final accessory in place.

Index and Directory of Designer Sources and Showrooms

You have probably noticed that "Sources" are listed at the end of each story of a designer interior in the center section of this book. Designers depend on these fine manufacturers and importers in order to orchestrate their interiors.

The sources listed in this directory are 1976 advertisers in *Residential Interiors* magazine. The magazine annually undertakes to create this useful guide for its readership of professional interior designers. Most of the sources listed sell exclusively to and through interior designers.

This directory is in three parts:

The Index Key to Product Sources
The Key will quickly tell you and your designer where to look for sources of the product you need. Both general and specific categories of products are listed in alphabetical order, along with references to the pages listing sources of that product.

The Index to Sources of Products
The Product Index will tell you and your designer the names of the companies who supply the type of product you are looking for. Also, beside the specific category titles, you will find references to the pages in the book where examples of that product are shown.

The Index to the Location of Sources
The Source Index lists sources in alphabetical order, giving the location and telephone number of the home office and some of the company's major showrooms or representatives across the nation. If there seems to be no showroom in your area, your designer can call or write the company's home office for information on the outlet nearest you.

Section 1 Index Key to Product Sources

GENERAL CATEGORIES

135 Accessories
135 Antiques
135 Bath
135–136 Beds & Bedding
136 Building Products
136 Equipment & Fixtures
136 Fabrics
136–137 Floor & Floor Coverings
137–138 Furniture
138–139 Lamps & Lighting
139 Services
139 Wallcoverings
139 Window Treatments

SPECIFIC CATEGORIES

A
135 Acrylic Accessories
137 Acrylic Furniture
136 Accordion Doors
136 Acoustical Ceiling Systems
136 Acoustical Ceiling Tile
136 Acoustical Partitions
137 Aluminum Furniture
135 Antique Art Objects
137 Antique Furniture
138 Architectural Lighting
139 Architectural Woodwork
136 Area & Accent Rugs
135 Art
139 Austrian Blinds

B
137 Bamboo Furniture
135 Bath Accessories
135 Bed Frames
135 Bedspreads
136 Box Springs
135 Bowls, Bidets
137 Brass Furniture
136 Bricks

C
138 Candelabras
139 Carpet & Rug Cleaners
136 Carpet Backing

136 Carpet Cleaning Supplies
136 Carpet Underlay and Supplies
136 Carpeting
136 Casements and Sheers
137 Ceramic Tile, Floor
139 Ceramic Tile, Wall
138 Chandeliers
135 Charts
135 Chinaware
137 Chrome Furniture
135 Clocks
137 Contemporary Furniture
138 Contemporary Lamps
136 Convertibles
137 Cork Tile, Floor
139 Cork Wallcovering
136 Curtain and Drapery Hardware
137 Cushion Filling Material
139 Custom Cabinetwork
137 Custom Woven Rugs

D
135 Decorative Hardware
135 Decorative Screens
136 Doors and Door Frames
136 Drapery Fabrics
139 Drapery Workrooms
139 Dyeing and Finishing

E
137 Early American Furniture
137 English Furniture

F
139 Fabric Finishing (Flameproofing, Backings, Stainproofing)
139 Felt Wallcovering
137 Fibers for Carpeting
135 Figures and Figurines
135 Fireplace Accessories
136 Fireplaces
139 Floor Stenciling
137 Folding Chairs
137 Folding Tables
137 French Furniture
137 Furniture Frames

G
136 Glass, Decorative or Patterned
139 Glass Tile, Wall
135 Globes
135 Graphics
136 Grilles

H
136 Headboards
137 Hi-Fi and Stereo Equipment

I
137 Italian Furniture

J
137 Juvenile Furniture

K
137 Kitchen Cabinets

L
138 Lamps
139 Lamp Shades
136 Leather
138 Light Bulbs, Decorative
139 Luminous Ceilings

M
136 Mantels
135 Maps
136 Marble
137 Marble Flooring
139 Matchstick Blinds
136 Mattresses
139 Metal Tile, Wall
138 Mirrored Furniture
135 Mirrors and Mirror Frames
136 Moldings
136 Movable Partitions

O
137 Occasional Tables
138 Oriental Furniture
137 Oriental Rugs
136 Ornamental Metal
138 Outdoor Furniture

P
135 Paintings/Prints
136 Panels/Paneling
137 Parquet Wood Tile
139 Photomurals
135 Picture Frames
135 Pillows, Decorative
135 Plants and Flowers, Artificial
135 Planters, Indoor
135 Planters, Outdoor
135 Plumbing Fixtures
136 Plywoods

Q
139 Quilting

R
138 Rattan Furniture
138 Reclining Chairs
138 Reproduction of Period Furniture
137 Resilient Sheet Vinyls, Floor
139 Roman Shades
137 Rubber Tile, Floor
136 Rugs, area and accent

S
138 Scandinavian Furniture
139 Sconces
136 Screens
136 Screen-Printed Fabrics (Custom)
135 Sculpture
140 Shades, Window
135 Silverware
136 Slate
136 Sofa Beds
138 Spanish Furniture
136 Stained Glass
137 Stainless Steel Furniture

136 Stair Railings, Metal, Rope, etc.
136 Stationary Partitions

T
135 Tapestries
139 Textile Wallcoverings (paper-backed)
135 Tiles, Bath
139 Track Lighting
139 Trade Buildings and Marts
139 Traditional Lamps
135 Tubs

U
138 Upholstered Furniture
139 Upholstering

V
140 Venetian Blinds
140 Vertical Blinds
135 Vases
136 Veneers
137 Vinyl Asbestos Tile, Floor
136 Vinyls
137 Vinyl Tile, Floor
139 Vinyl Wallcoverings

W
139 Wall Carpeting
139 Wallcovering Murals
135 Wall Hangings
139 Wallcoverings and Matching Fabrics
139 Wallpapers
135 Wall Plaques
138 Wall Systems (Shelving & Storage)
138 Wicker Furniture
138 Wood Desks
137 Wood Flooring
140 Wood Shutters (Louvered, Grille)
136 Woods
140 Woven Wood Blinds and Shades
138 Wrought-Iron Furniture

These sources are for the exclusive use of your designer.

Section 2 Index to Sources of Products

Hastings Tile & "Il Bagno"
  Collection
Kirsch Company
Plexability Ltd.
Sherle Wagner International

Plumbing Fixtures, 27, 101

Donghia, Inc.
Hastings Tile & "Il Bagno"
  Collection
Sherle Wagner International

Tiles, 27

Country Floors, Inc.
Donghia, Inc.
Hastings Tile & "Il Bagno"
  Collection
House of Quarry Ltd.
Sherle Wagner International

Tubs, Bidets, Bowls, 26, 27, 101

Donghia, Inc.
Hastings Tile & "Il Bagno"
  Collection
Sherle Wagner International

BEDS & BEDDING

Bed Frames, 10, 69, 110

A & D Interiors, Inc.
Atelier International, Ltd.
Avery Boardman Ltd.
Bedquarters
Design Center of New Jersey
Four Corners
ICF, Inc.
The George J. Kempler Co., Inc.
Liquid Sleep Interiors
The Pace Collection
Smith & Watson
Southeast Wholesale Furniture Co.
John Stuart Inc./John Widdicomb
  Co.
Swan Brass Beds
Vanleigh Furniture Showrooms

Bedspreads, 54, 60, 63, 80, 110,
122

Avanti Designs
Bedquarters
Al Burkhardt Custom Shade Co.
Design Center of New Jersey
Fabindia, Inc.
Kirsch Company
Liquid Sleep Interiors
Nettle Creek Industries
F. Schumacher & Co.
Showroom III/Haitian Cotton
Siesta Bedding Co.
Weavers Domain Ltd./Window
  Modes, Inc.
Window Works Unlimited

Box Springs & Mattresses, 91,
98, 108

A & D Interiors, Inc.
Avery Boardman Ltd.
Baker, Knapp & Tubbs
Bedquarters
Design Center of New Jersey
A. T. Euster Furniture Co.
Fabric Quilters Unlimited, Inc.
Foremost Furniture
The George J. Kempler Co., Inc.
John Mascheroni, Inc.
Southeast Wholesale Furniture Co.
John Stuart Inc./John Widdicomb
  Co.
Vanleigh Furniture Showrooms

Convertibles, 8, 38, 124

A & D Interiors, Inc.
Avery Boardman Ltd.
Bedquarters
A. T. Euster Furniture Co.
ICF, Inc.

The Pace Collection
Southeast Wholesale Furniture Co.
John Stuart Inc./John Widdicomb
  Co.
Swan Brass Beds
Vanleigh Furniture Showrooms

Headboards, 23, 63, 102, 105

A & D Interiors, Inc.
Atelier International, Ltd.
Avery Boardman Ltd.
Baker, Knapp & Tubbs
Bedquarters
Customwood
A. T. Euster Furniture Co.
Four Corners
ICF, Inc.
The George J. Kempler Co., Inc.
John Mascheroni, Inc.
The Pace Collection
Plexability Ltd.
Sieberts, Cox & L'Herisson, Inc.
Siesta Bedding Co.
Smith & Watson
Southeast Wholesale Furniture Co.
John Stuart Inc./John Widdicomb
  Co.
Swan Brass Beds
Tri-Mark Designs
Trouvailles, Inc.
Vanleigh Furniture Showrooms
Wood and Hogan, Inc.

Sofa Beds, 8, 38

A & D Interiors, Inc.
Atelier International, Ltd.
Avery Boardman Ltd.
Baker, Knapp & Tubbs
Bedquarters
Beylerian
Cavallon Associates, Inc.
Classic Gallery, Inc.
Corsican
Design Center of New Jersey
A. T. Euster Furniture Co.
Foremost Furniture
ICF, Inc.
The George J. Kempler Co., Inc.
The Pace Collection
Southeast Wholesale Furniture Co.
John Stuart Inc./John Widdicomb
  Co.
Swan Brass Beds
Trouvailles, Inc.
Vanleigh Furniture Showrooms

BUILDING PRODUCTS

Accordion Doors, 124

Customwood
Weavers Domain Ltd./Window
  Modes, Inc.

Acoustical Ceiling Systems

Bangkok Industries, Inc.
Design Center of New Jersey

Acoustical Ceiling Tile

Bangkok Industries, Inc.
Design Center of New Jersey

Acoustical Partitions

Knoll International
Joe Sherry Associates, Inc.

Doors and Door Frames, 89, 98,
112

Customwood

Fireplaces and Mantels, 60, 85,
94, 95, 116, 120–121, 126

Focal Point, Inc.
International Terra Cotta, Inc.
John Stuart Inc./John Widdicomb
  Co.

Glass, Decorative or Patterned, 8

I. Schwartz Glass & Mirror Co.

Marble, Slate and Bricks, 26, 60,
100, 112

Joe Sherry Associates, Inc.
Sherle Wagner International

Moldings, 52, 85, 94, 110

Focal Point, Inc.
Old World Moulding & Finishing,
  Inc.

Movable Partitions, 58, 124

Joe Sherry Associates, Inc.
Customwood

Ornamental Metal, 8, 89

Armento, Inc.
Meadowcraft-B'ham Ornamental
  Iron Co.

Panels/Paneling, 60, 76, 83, 84,
94, 95, 120–121

Cado/Royal System, Inc.
Customwood
Inwil International Corp.
Masonite Corporation
Old World Moulding & Finishing,
  Inc.
Joe Sherry Associates, Inc.

Screens and Grilles, 60, 94, 95

Customwood
Design Center of New Jersey
Ohline Corporation
Old World Moulding & Finishing,
  Inc.

Stained Glass

Edward J. Byrne Studio
Michael Ohnmacht Stained Glass
  Studio

Stair Railings, Metal, Rope, etc.,
83

Bangkok Industries, Inc.
Old World Moulding & Finishing,
  Inc.

Stationary Partitions, 89, 129

Customwood

Woods, Veneers, Plywoods, 84

Bangkok Industries, Inc.
Customwood

EQUIPMENT & FIXTURES

Curtain and Drapery Hardware,
102–103

Design Center of New Jersey
Fabric Quilters Unlimited, Inc.
Walker Manufacturing Company

FABRICS

Casements and Sheers, 12, 14, 62,
75

Brunschwig & Fils, Inc.

Henry Cassen, Inc.
Charterhouse Designs Ltd.
Design Center of New Jersey
Donghia, Inc.
Fabindia, Inc.
S. Harris & Co., Inc.
S. M. Hexter Company
Knoll International
Krupnick Bros., Inc.
Jack Lenor Larsen, Inc.
Arthur H. Lee & Jofa, Inc.
Andre Matenciot Co., Inc.
Odenheimer & Baker, Inc.
Scalamandré
F. Schumacher & Co.
Joe Sherry Associates, Inc.
Stroheim & Romann
Unika-Vaev USA, Inc.
Albert Van Luit & Co.

Drapery and Upholstery Fabrics,
12, 13, 14, 15, 18–25, 37, 58,
60, 61, 62, 63, 68, 69, 74, 76, 78,
79, 82, 84, 85, 89, 90, 92, 100,
102, 103, 105, 108, 109, 111,
115, 119, 121, 122, 124

American Enka Co.
Atelier International, Ltd.
Baker, Knapp & Tubbs
Boussac of France, Inc.
Brunschwig & Fils, Inc.
Charterhouse Designs Ltd.
Design Center of New Jersey
Donghia, Inc.
Eisenhart Wallcoverings Co.
Fabindia, Inc.
S. Fankash, Inc.
First Editions, Inc.
S. Harris & Co., Inc.
S. M. Hexter Company
India Nepal, Inc.
Knoll International
Krupnick Bros., Inc.
Jack Lenor Larsen, Inc.
Eric Lauren
Arthur H. Lee & Jofa, Inc.
Margowen, Inc.
Andre Matenciot Co., Inc.
Nettle Creek Industries
Odenheimer & Baker, Inc.
The Pace Collection
Portico Fabrics
Quadrille
Reed Wallcovering
Scalamandré
F. Schumacher & Co.
Joe Sherry Associates, Inc.
Shrowroom III/Haitian Cotton
Stendig, Inc.
Stroheim & Romann
John Stuart Inc./John Widdicomb
  Co.
Richard E. Thibaut, Inc.
Turner, Ltd.
Unika-Vaev USA, Inc.
Albert Van Luit & Co.

Leather, 60, 62, 63, 89, 90–91,
110, 113, 116, 123

Atelier International, Ltd.
Baker, Knapp & Tubbs
Campaniello Imports, Ltd.
Design Center of New Jersey
Donghia, Inc.
Eros Leather Furniture, Inc.
S. Harris & Co., Inc.
S. M. Hexter Company
Knoll International
Krupnick Bros., Inc.
Jack Lenor Larsen, Inc.
Arthur H. Lee & Jofa, Inc.
The Pace Collection
Odenheimer & Baker, Inc.
Scalamandré
F. Schumacher & Co.
Stendig, Inc.
Stroheim & Romann
Unika-Vaev USA, Inc.

Screen Printed Fabrics (Custom),
21

Design Center of New Jersey
Donghia, Inc.
First Editions, Inc.
S. Harris & Co., Inc.

These sources are for the exclusive use of your designer.

These sources are for the exclusive use of your designer.

Section 3 Index to the Location of Sources

*Home offices are marked by an asterisk

A

A & D INTERIORS, INC., 192 Lexington Ave., New York, NY 10016, 212/ 889-7151

AMBIENCE ACCESSORIES, INC. 979 Third Ave., Suite 1720, New York, NY 10022, 212/ 688-0170

AMERICAN ENKA CORPORATION, 530 Fifth Ave., New York, NY 10036, 212/ 486-0327

ARGO & COMPANY, INC., 182 Ezell St., Drawer 2747, Spartanburg, SC 29304, 803/ 583-9766

ARMENTO, INC., 1011 Military Rd., Buffalo, NY 14217, 716/ 875-2423

ART FOR ART'S SAKE, 253-13 Northern Blvd., Little Neck, NY 11362, 212/ 423-2392

ATELIER INTERNATIONAL, LTD.
Atlanta—MacKerer, Walker, Graham, 19 Fourteenth St., N.W.
Boston—Montage, 420 Boylston Street
Chicago—Atelier Int'l Ltd., 1011 Merchandise Mart
Dallas—Atelier Int'l Ltd., 608 World Trade Center
Los Angeles—Fortress Collections, 8801 Beverly Blvd.
Miami—Lloyd Smith & Mackerer, Walker, Graham, 276 N.E. 67 St.
*New York—595 Madison Ave., New York, NY 10022, 212/ 644-0400
Philadelphia—Benjamin Buchbinder Assoc., 1019 Hartranft Ave., Ft. Washington
San Francisco—David White, 137 Divisadero St.

ATLANTA DECORATIVE ARTS CENTER, 351 Peachtree Hills Ave., N.E., Atlanta, GA 30305, 404/ 688-8994

AUFFRAY & CO.,
Atlanta—Hugh Cochran, 351 Peachtree Hills Ave., N.E.
Chicago—Patterson, Flynn & Martin, 1226 Merchandise Mart
Dallas—Gerald Hargett, 220 Decorative Center
Los Angeles—C. W. Stockwell, 320 N. Madison Ave.
*New York—146 E. 56 St., New York, NY 10022, 212/ 753-3931

AVAKIAN BROTHERS, INC., 10 W. 33 St., New York, NY 10001, 212/ 947-9711

AVANTI DESIGNS, 979 Third Ave., 800N New York, NY 10022, 212/ 486-9696

AVERY BOARDMAN LTD.
Miami—LaVerne Galleries, 3925 N. Miami Ave.
*New York—979 Third Ave., New York, NY 10022, 212/ 688-6611
Philadelphia—Avery Boardman Ltd., 2400 Market St.

B

B & B AMERICA
Boston—Montage, 420 Boylston Street
Los Angeles—8919 Beverly Blvd.
*New York—745 Fifth Ave., New York, NY 10022, 212/ 752-5234
San Francisco—B & B America, 210 The Icehouse

BAKER, KNAPP & TUBBS
Atlanta—351 Peachtree Hills Ave., N.E.
*Chicago—474 Merchandise Mart, Chicago, IL, 60654, 312/ 337-7144
Dallas—150 Decorative Center
High Point, N.C.—319 Hamilton St.
Los Angeles—8687 Melrose Ave.
Miami—7321 N.E. Second Ave.
New York—979 Third Ave.
Philadelphia—2400 Market St.
San Francisco—848 Battery St.

BANGKOK INDUSTRIES, INC.
Atlanta—George D. Bridges Co., 4732 Stone Dr.
Chicago—Thailand Teakwood Importers, Inc., 645 N. Michigan Ave.
Dallas—French-Brown Distributors, 6852 Twins Hills Ave.
Los Angeles—Builders Flooring Service, Inc., 2603 San Fernando Rd.
New York—Designed Wood Flooring Center, 940 Third Ave.
*Philadelphia—1900 S. 20th St. Philadelphia, PA 19145, 215/ 334-1500

BARKHORDARIAN, 101 Kansas St., San Francisco, CA 94103, 415/ 861-0907

BEDQUARTERS, 964 Third Ave., New York, NY 10022, 212/ 371-6355

BEYLERIAN LIMITED, 305 E. 63 St., New York, NY 10021, 212/ 755-6300

VOJTECH BLAU, 980 Madison Ave., New York, NY 10021, 212/ 249-4525

BOUSSAC OF FRANCE, INC.
Atlanta—Hugh Cochran Assoc., 351 Peachtree Hills Ave., N.E.
Chicago—Patterson, Flynn & Martin, 404 N. Wells
Dallas—Decorators Walk, 250 Decorative Center
Los Angeles—Edward Fields, Inc., 8950 Beverly Blvd.
Miami—Carousel Designs, Inc., 35 N.E. 40 St.
*New York—979 Third Ave., New York, NY 10022, 212/ 421-0534
Philadelphia—D & E Showrooms, 2400 Market St.
San Francisco—Zuckerman Fabrics, 101 Kansas St.

LOUIS W. BOWEN, INC.
Boston—Devon Service, 420 Boylston Street
Chicago—T. V. Betterman, 611 Merchandise Mart
Dallas—Bert Pedlar, 2611 Fairmount
Los Angeles—Keith McCoy & Assoc., 8710 Melrose Ave.
Miami—Bob Collins, Inc., 120 N.E. 39 St.
*New York—979 Third Ave., New York, NY 10022, 212/ 392-5810
Philadelphia—Bob Collins, Inc., 1606 Walnut St.
San Francisco—Winfield Winsor, 458 Jackson Sq.

BOYD LIGHTING COMPANY
Atlanta—Paul B. Raulet, Inc., 351 Peachtree Hills, N.E.
Boston—M-Geough Robinson, 420 Boylston Street
Chicago—Patterson, Flynn & Martin, Suite 1226, Merchandise Mart
Dallas—E. C. Dicken, 480 Decorative Center
Los Angeles—Kneedler-Fauchere, 8687 Melrose Ave.
Miami—Decorators Walk, 3825 N.E. First Court
New York—Luten, Clarey & Stern, 1059 Third Ave.
Philadelphia—Darr-Luck, 2400 Market St.
*San Francisco—56 12 St. San Francisco, CA 94103, 415/ 431-4300
Showroom—Kneedler-Fauchere, 101 Kansas St.

BRUNSCHWIG & FILS, INC.
Atlanta—Atlanta Decorative Arts Center, 351 Peachtree Hills Ave., N.E.
Boston—E. Wells McLean, 420 Boylston Street
Chicago—6168 Merchandise Mart
Dallas—410 Decorative Center
Los Angeles—653 Pacific Design Center
*New York—979 Third Ave., New York, NY 10022, 212/ 838-7878
Philadelphia—A. F. Brown, The Marketplace, Suite 201, 2400 Market St.
San Francisco—Regency House, 407 Jackson Sq.

AL BURKHARDT CUSTOM SHADE CO., 1152 Second Ave., New York, NY 10021, 212/ 688-3095

EDWARD J. BYRNE STUDIO, 135 Cherry La., Doylestown, PA, 18901 215/ 348-2577

C

CADO/ROYAL SYSTEM INC.
Atlanta—MWG, 19 Fourteenth St., N.W.
Boston—Montage, 420 Boylston Street
Chicago—Charles Orr, 1711 Merchandise Mart
Los Angeles—Pacific Design Center, 8687 Melrose Ave.
Miami MWG, 276 N.E. 67 St.
New York—979 Third Ave., Lobby "N"
San Francisco—Ed Johnson, 151 Union Street
*Woodside, NY—57-08 39 Ave., Woodside, NY 11377, 212/ 478-5400

CAHILL-RUBEN LTD., 101 Kansas St., San Francisco, CA 94103, 415/ 621-3018

CAMPANIELLO IMPORTS LTD., 665 Fifth Ave., New York, NY 10022, 212/ 371-3700

CASA BELLA IMPORTS
Atlanta—Designer Products Ltd., ADAC Space 49, 351 Peachtree Hills Ave., N.E.
Chicago—Richard Himmel Design Pavilion, 219 W. Erie St.
Dallas—Waitman Martin, 1444 Oak Lawn Ave.
Los Angeles—Casa Bella International, Pacific Design Ctr., 8687 Melrose Ave., Suite 504
*Miami—3750 Biscayne Blvd., Miami, FL 33137, 305/ 573-0804
New York—John Mascheroni, 979 Third Ave.
Philadelphia—Rodal Design Collection, The Marketplace, 2400 Market St.
San Francisco—Kneedler-Fauchere, 101 Kansas St.

CASA TALAMANTES, 117 N. Awbrey, El Paso, TX 79905, 915/ 772-3711

HENRY CASSEN, INC.
Atlanta—Decorators Walk, 351 Peachtree Hills Ave., N.E.
Boston—Decorators Walk, 420 Boylston Street
Chicago—Betterman's, 611 Merchandise Mart
Dallas—Decorators Walk, 250 Decorative Center
Los Angeles—Decorators Walk, 131 N. Robertson Blvd.
Miami—Decorators Walk, 3825 N.E. 1st Court
*New York—979 Third Ave., New York, NY 10022, 212/ 684-2000
Philadelphia—Decorators Walk, 2400 Market St.
San Francisco—Decorators Walk, 101 Kansas St.

CASTELLI FURNITURE
Atlanta—Designer Products Ltd, ADAC, Space 49, 351 Peachtree Hills Ave., N.E.
Chicago—Castelli Furniture, 1150 Merchandise Mart
Dallas—W. Glen Hennings, 605 World Trade Center
Los Angeles—Fortress, Incorporated, 8801 Beverly Blvd.
*New York—950 Third Ave., New York, NY 10022, 212/ 751-2050

CAVALLON ASSOCIATES, INC., 979 Third Ave., New York, NY 10022, 212/ 753-3377

CHARTERHOUSE DESIGNS LTD.
Atlanta—Culpepper/Osborne, 351 Peachtree Hills Ave.
Boston—Berkeley House, 420 Boylston Street
Chicago—Michael Roberts, 325 N. Wells St.
Dallas—John Edward Hughes, Inc., 100 Oak Lawn Plaza
Los Angeles—Jay Clark, 110 S. Robertson Blvd.
Miami—Atrium Handprints, 50 N.E. 40 St.
*New York—979 Third Ave., New York, NY 10022, 212/ 752-4664
Philadelphia—Matches, Inc., 2400 Market St.
San Francisco—Wall-Pride, 1035 Battery St.

CHRISTEN, INC., 59 Branch St., St. Louis, MO 63147, 314/ 241-7033

CHRISTOPHER PRINTS, INC., 134 Sand Park Rd., Cedar Grove, NJ 07009, 212/ 239-6600

CLASSIC GALLERY, INC.
Chicago—Max Futorian, 1680 Merchandise Mart
*High Point—2009 Fulton Pl., High Point, NC 27263, 919/ 886-4191
Showroom—Wrenn Comm. Bldg.

FREDERICK COOPER LAMPS
*Chicago—2545 W. Diversey Ave., Chicago, IL 60647, 312/ 384-0800
Showroom—1214 Merchandise Mart
Dallas—1012 Dallas Trade Mart
Los Angeles—418 L.A. Furniture Mart
New York—Merchandise Mart, 41 Madison Ave.
San Francisco—569 Western Merchandise Mart

CORSICAN, 243/ E. 24 St., Los Angeles, CA 90058, 213/ 587-3101

COUNTRY FLOORS INC.
Chicago—Hispanic Designs, 6125 N. Cicero Ave.
Dallas—French-Brown Floors, 7007 Greenville Ave.
Los Angeles—Kneedler-Fauchere, Pacific Design Center, 8687 Melrose Ave.
Miami—Country Floors, 82 N.E. 40 St.
*New York—300 E. 61 St., New York, NY 10021, 212/ 758-7414
Philadelphia—Country Floors, 1706 Locust St.
San Francisco—Kneedler-Fauchere, 101 Kansas St.

COSCO CONTEMPORARIES, 2525 State St., Columbus, IN 47201, 812/ 372-0141

CRAFTSMEN'S FURNITURE CO., 12415 N.E. 13 Ave., No. Miami, FL 33161, 305/ 891-9172

CROWN WALLCOVERING CORP., 979 Third Ave., New York, NY 10022, 212/ 421-6550

CUSTOMWOOD, 4840 Pan American Freeway, N.E., Albuquerque, NM 87109, 505/ 344-1691

D

DECORATIVE ARTS CENTER, 305 E. 63 St., New York, NY 10021, 212/ 838-7736

DESIGN CENTER OF NEW JERSEY, 1081 Bristol Rd., Mountainside, NJ 07092, 201/ 654-3040

DESIGN GALLERIES, INC., 325 N. Wells St., Chicago, IL 60610, 312/ 644-5860

DEUTSCH, INC.
Los Angeles—426 So. Robertson
*New York—196 Lexington Ave., New York, NY 10016, 212/ 683-8746

DOME FURNITURE SHOWROOM, 8104 Beverly Blvd., Los Angeles, CA 90048, 213/ 653-5830

DONGHIA, INC.
Los Angeles—8715 Melrose Ave.
*New York—315 E. 62 St., New York, NY 10021, 212/838-9100

DUBOSE ARCHITECTURAL FLOORING, 905 San Pedro Ave., San Antonio, TX 78212, 512/ 225-2844

DURACLEAN INTERNATIONAL, Deerfield, IL 60015, 312/ 945-2000

DUTCH PRODUCTS & S CO., S. Main St., Yardley, PA 19067, 215/ 493-4873

E

EAGLESHAM PRINTS, INC.
Atlanta—Hugh Cochran, 351 Peachtree Ave., NE
Boston—George & Frances Davison, 420 Boylston Street
Chicago—John Strauss, 160 E. Erie St.
Dallas—Gerald Hargett, Inc., 220 Decorative Ctr.
Los Angeles—Directional West, 8687 Melrose Ave.
Miami—Hugh Cochran, 1 N.E. 40 St.
*New York—979 Third Ave., New York, NY 10022, 212/ 759-2060
Philadelphia—JW Showroom, 2400 Market St.
San Francisco—Lawrence/Green, 151 Union Street.

EATON-PROVOST IMPORTS CORP
*Arcade, NY—RD #2, East Arcade Rd., Arcade, NY 14009, 716/ 496-7266
Chicago—Mike Bell, Inc., 220 W. Kinzie St.
San Francisco—Manor House Assocs., The Show Place, 2 Kansas St.

EISENHART WALLCOVERINGS CO.
*Hanover, PA—Pine St., Hanover, PA 17331, 717/ 632-5918
High Point—Hunter & Co., 1945 W. Green Dr.
Miami—Key Wallcovering, 100 N.W. 176 St.
Philadelphia—Northwestern Wallcovering, 1909 E. Washington Lane

EROS LEATHER FURNITURE, INC.
Atlanta—Designer Products Ltd., ADAC Space 49, 351 Peachtree Hills Ave., N.E.
Chicago—325 No. Wells St.
Dallas—J. Riley Smith, 505 Oak Lawn Plaza
High Point—Wrenn Comm. Building
Los Angeles—Peter Lang, Pacific Design Center, 8687 Melrose Ave.
*New York—488 Madison Ave., New York, NY 10022, 212/ 753-9740
San Francisco—James Kehoe Co., Galleria Design Center, 101 Kansas St.

EUROTEX, INC.
Atlanta—Designer Products Ltd., Space 49, 351 Peachtree Hills Ave.
Boston—Shep Brown Assoc., 27 Stanhope St.
Chicago—11-121 Merchandise Mart
Dallas—Edmund Kirk Assoc., Suite 604, Oak Lawn Plaza

Los Angeles—Epstein-Goman Assoc., 8201 Beverly Blvd., Suite 501
* Philadelphia—The Marketplace, 2400 Market St., Philadelphia, PA 19103, 215/ 546-5700
A. T. EUSTER FURNITURE CO., 3300 N.E. Second Ave., Miami, FL 33137, 305/ 573-3200

F

FABINDIA, INC.
* Canton, CT—Canton, CT 06019, 203/ 693-8551
Miami—Gateway International, John Dominici, Miami Merchandise Mart
FABRIC QUILTERS UNLIMITED, INC., 1400 Shames Dr., Westbury, NY 11590, 516/ 333-2866
EDWARD FIELDS, INC.
Atlanta—ADAC, 351 Peachtree Ave., N.E.
Boston—420 Boylston Street
Chicago—635 Merchandise Mart
Dallas—280 Decorative Center
Los Angeles—8850 Beverly Blvd.
Miami—50 N.E. 39 St.
* New York—232 E. 59 St., New York, NY 10022, 212/ 759-2200
FIRST EDITIONS WALLCOVERINGS AND FABRICS, INC.
Atlanta—Hugh Cochran, 351 Peachtree Ave., N.E.
Boston—George & Frances Davison, 420 Boylston Street
Chicago—Walter Associates, 400 N. Wells St.
Dallas—Claude Pendleton, Inc., 110 Oak Lawn Plaza
Los Angeles—J. Robert Scott, 8727 Melrose Ave.
Miami—Hugh Cochran, 1 N.E. 40 St.
* New York—979 Third Ave., New York, NY 10022, 212/ 355-1150
Philadelphia—JW Showroom, 2400 Market St.
San Francisco—Lawrence Green, 101 Kansas St.
FLOKATI IMPORTS, INC.
Atlanta—Robert Kelly & Assocs., 351 Peachtree Hills Ave., N.E.
Chicago—Andrew Sales Co., 13175 Merchandise Mart
Dallas—Wm. P. O'Brien, 3024 Dallas Trade Mart
* New York—Suite 2001, 730 Fifth Ave., New York, NY 10019, 212/ 757-4024
Philadelphia—Maen Showroom Ltd., 2400 Market St.
San Francisco—Fur Design Interiors, 1355 Market St.
FOCAL POINT, INC., 3760 Lower Roswell Rd., Marietta, GA 30067, 404/ 971-7172
FOREMOST FURNITURE, 8 W. 30 St., New York, NY 10001, 212/ 889-6347
FOUR CORNERS, 1250 W. Washington, Columbus, IN 47201, 812/ 372-2553
BERNARD FREDRICK, INC., 2400 Market St., Philadelphia, PA 19103, 215/ 567-0667

G

GABRIEL CUSTOM FURNITURE CO., 31-49 12 St., Long Island City, NY 11106, 212/ 728-6097
NAOMI GALE/SHELVES UNLIMITED
Atlanta—George Cox Assocs., 351 Peachtree Hills Ave., N.E.
* Bronx, NY—2400 Ryer Ave., Bronx, NY 10458, 212/298-7088
Dallas—I. H. Pritchard, Inc., 670 World Trade Center
Los Angeles—de Benedictis Showrooms, 8745 W. 3 St.
Miami—Blake-Preville, Inc., 4302 N.E. 2nd Ave.
New York—Naomi Gale, 233 E. 59 St.
San Francisco—de Benedictis Showrooms, 151 Union St.
GALLERIA MOBILI, 976 Third Ave., New York, NY 10022, 212/ 688-7444
GEORGIAN ART LIGHTING DESIGNS, INC., P.O. Box 325, Lawrenceville, GA 30246, 404/ 963-6221
THE GALLERIA DESIGN CENTER, 101 Kansas St., San Francisco, CA 94103, 415/ 864-1500
HARRY GITLIN, INC., 305 E. 60 St., New York, NY 10022, 212/ 751-7130
PHILIP GRAF WALLPAPERS, INC.
Atlanta—McCormack Assoc., 351 Peachtree Hills Ave., N.E.
Boston—George & Frances Davison, 420 Boylston Street
Chicago—Warner Co., 6-134 Merchandise Mart
Dallas—Gerald Hargett, Inc., 220 Decorative Center

H

HANNO, INC.
Chicago—Intergroup Collections, 1209 Merchandise Mart
Dallas—Ernest Low & Assoc., 611 World Trade Ctr.
* Elkhart, IN—2400 Sterling Ave., Elkhart, IN 46514, 219/ 293-1812
Miami—Joseph Schmidt, Inc., 3911 N.E. First Ave.
New York—A. Blank, Inc., 88 Broad St.
Philadelphia—Marden Assoc., Plaza 16, E. Lancaster Ave.
San Francisco—CDI, 315 Pacific Ave.
HARMIL CARPET CO., 336 E. 60 St., New York, NY 10021, 212/ 838-1330
HARMONY CARPET
Atlanta—McCormack & Co., 351 Peachtree Hills Ave., N.E.
Boston—George & Frances Davison, 420 Boylston Street
Chicago—Watson-Smith, 6-127 Merchandise Mart
Dallas—Gerald Hargett, Inc., 220 Decorative Center
Los Angeles—J. Robert Scott, 8727 Melrose Ave.
Miami—Berven Carpets Corp., 63 N.E. 40 St.
* New York—979 Third Ave., New York, NY 10022, 212/ 355-6000
San Francisco—Nevins & Pearson Assoc., 151 Union St.
S. HARRIS & CO., INC.
Chicago—Nick Karas, 1374 Mdse. Mart
Dallas—S. Harris, 1444 Oak Lawn Ave., Suite 114
* El Segundo, CA—580 S. Douglas St., El Segundo, CA 90245, 213/ 973-7402
Los Angeles—S. Harris, 123 N. Robertson Blvd.
Miami—Jerry Pair & Assoc., Inc., 105 N.E. 39 St.
New York—Allume, 979 Third Ave.
Philadelphia—Duncan-Huggins, 1704 Walnut
San Francisco—S. Harris, 451 Jackson Sq.
HARRISON-VAN HORN
Atlanta—Donohue & Travis, Inc., 351 Peachtree Hills Ave., N.E.
Chicago—Michael Roberts, Inc., 325 No. Wells St.
Dallas—E. C. Dicken, 480 Decorative Center
* Los Angeles—1119 So. La Brea Ave., Los Angeles, CA 90019, 213/ 933-7476
Showroom—Kneedler-Fauchere, Pacific Design Center
Miami—39 East, 90 N.E. 39th St.
New York—Paul Jones, Inc., 979 Third Ave.
Philadelphia—Duncan-Huggins Ltd., 1704 Walnut Ave.
San Francisco—Kneedler-Fauchere, 101 Kansas St.
HASTINGS TILE & "II BAGNO" COLLECTION
Atlanta—Apex Supply Co., Inc., 2500 Button Gwinnett Dr.
* New York—964 Third Ave., New York, NY 10022, 212/ 755-2710
San Francisco—Pacific Coast Products & Designers Products West, 101 Kansas St., Space 270G
S. M. HEXTER COMPANY
Atlanta—35 ADAC, 351 Peachtree Hills Ave., N.E.
Boston—420 Boylston Street
* Cleveland, OH—2800 Superior Ave., Cleveland, OH 44114, 216/ 696-0146
Dallas—William Bass, 300 Decorative Center
Los Angeles—143 N. Robertson Blvd.
Miami—94 N.E. 40th St.
Philadelphia—1606 Walnut St.
San Francisco—440 Jackson St.
HOUSE OF QUARRY LTD., 1544 Northern Blvd., Manhasset, NY 11030, 516/ 627-4805
HOUSE OF SPAIN & TROUVEZ L'EUROPE, 315 E. 62 St., New York, NY 10021, 212/ 243-4075

I

ICF, INC.
Boston—27 Stanhope Street

Chicago—1010 Merchandise Mart
Los Angeles—8899 Beverly Blvd.
* New York—145 E. 57. St., New York, NY 10022, 212/ 752-5870
San Francisco—151 Union St.
IMPERIAL IMAGINEERING LTD.
Atlanta—McCormack & Assoc. Decorative Arts Ctr.
Chicago—Crown Lamp Co., American Merchandise Mart
Dallas—Sparks Assoc., 2502 Cedar Springs at Fairmont
High Point—Classica Workshops
Los Angeles—Rockwell-West, Inc., LA Home Furn. Mart
* Niles, IL—7412 N. Milwaukee Ave., Niles, IL 60648, 312/ 647-8530
Philadelphia—Taube, Inc., 2317 Chestnut St.
INDIA NEPAL, INC.
Atlanta—Bobby Hendrick & Assoc., Atlanta Mdse. Mt.
Chicago—India Nepal, 412 N. Orleans St.
Dallas—Stanley Beard Assoc., 2119 Dallas Trade Mt.
Los Angeles—Brack Shops, 527 W. 7 St.
Miami—1AA51 Mdse Mart
* New York—233 Fifth Ave., New York, NY 10016, 212/ 481-1300
INSTOCK PAPERS, INC.
Atlanta—Hugh Cochran, 351 Peachtree Hills Ave., N.E.
Boston—George & Frances Davison, 420 Boylston Street
Chicago—John Strauss Int'l, 160 E. Erie St.
Dallas—Gerald Hargett Inc., 220 Decorative Ctr.
Los Angeles—J. Robert Scott & Assoc., 8727 Melrose Ave.
Miami—Hugh Cochran, 1 N.E. 40 St.
* New York—979 Third Ave., New York, NY 10022, 212/ 826-6417
Philadelphia—JW Showroom, Space 304, 2400 Market St.
San Francisco—Lawrence/Green Ltd., 101 Kansas St.
INTERNATIONAL TERRA COTTA, INC.
Atlanta—Designer Products Ltd., 351 Peachtree Hills Ave., N.E.
Dallas—International Terra Cotta, Oak Lawn Plaza, Space 308
* Los Angeles—690 N. Robertson Blvd., Los Angeles, CA 90069, 213/ 657-3752
INTERPACE CORPORATION, FRANCISCAN
Atlanta—Wenczel Tile Co. of Florida, 3118 Oakcliff Industrial
Chicago—Brann Clay Products Co., 12430 S. Kedvale Ave.
Dallas—American Tile Supply, Inc., 8105 Sovereign Row
* Los Angeles—2901 Los Feliz Blvd., Los Angeles, CA 90039, 213/ 663-3361
Miami—Dunan Brick Yards Showroom, 84 N.E. 40 St.
New York—Architectural Material Center, 101 Park Ave.
San Francisco—Dillon Tile Supply, Inc., 2765—16 St.
INVINCIBLE PARLOR FRAME CO., 11-13 Maryland Ave., Paterson, NJ 07503, 201/ 274-7440
INWIL INTERNATIONAL CORP., 31-49 12 St., Long Island City, NY 11106, 212/ 721-2909

J

JANUS DESIGNS, INC., 979 Third Ave., New York, NY 10022, 212/ 754-4422
JASPER CABINET CO.
Atlanta—Atlanta Merchandise Mart, Peachtree & Harris, Space 20D-5B
Chicago—1780 Merchandise Mart
Dallas—Home Furniture Mart, Stemmons Expressway
High Point—Southern Furn. Exposition Bldg., 6-8 Green Wing
* Jasper, IN—P.O. Box 69, 126 So. Jackson St., Jasper, IN 47546, 812/ 482-4747
New York—N.Y. Furniture Exchange, 200 Lexington Ave.
San Francisco—Western Furniture Mt. #2, 1355 Market St.
JOANNA WESTERN MILLS CO.
Atlanta—2225 Faulkner Rd., N.E.
Boston—85 Bolton Street, Cambridge
* Chicago—2141 S. Jefferson St., Chicago, IL 60616, 312/ 226-3232
Showroom—1515 Louis St.
Dallas—Wm. Volker & Co., 1700 Cockrell Ave.
Los Angeles—2301 E. 7 St.
Miami—1001 N.W. 159 Dr.
San Francisco—475 Eccles Avenue

JONES AND ERWIN, INC., 232 E. 59 St., New York, NY 10022, 212/ 759-3706

K

THE GEORGE J. KEMPLER CO., INC., 160 Fifth Ave., New York, NY 10010, 212/ 989-1180
KIRSCH COMPANY
Atlanta—6025 LaGrange Blvd., S.W.
Chicago—1306 Merchandise Mart
Dallas—330—3 World Trade Center
Los Angeles—6021 S. Malt Ave.
Miami—15885 N.W. 13 Ave.
New York—261 Fifth Ave.
San Francisco—20427 Corsair Blvd.
* Sturgis, MI—309 N. Prospect St., Sturgis, MI 49091, 616/ 651-2311
KITTINGER COMPANY
Atlanta—ADAC, 351 Peachtree Hills Ave., N.E.
Boston—M-Geough Robinson, Inc., 420 Boylston Street
* Buffalo, NY—1893 Elmwood Ave., Buffalo, NY 14207, 716/ 876-1000
Chicago—6-158 Merchandise Mart
Dallas—E. C. Dicken, Inc., 480 Decorative Center
Los Angeles—Kneedler-Fauchere, 8687 Melrose Ave.
New York—DAC, 305 E. 63 St.
San Francisco—Nevins-Pearson Assoc., 151 Union St.
KNOLL INTERNATIONAL
Atlanta—225 Peachtree St., N.E.
Boston—100 Charles River Plaza
Chicago—1111 Merchandise Mart
Dallas—676 World Trade Center
Los Angeles—PDC, 8687 Melrose Ave.
* New York—745 Fifth Ave., New York, NY 10022, 212/ 826-2400
Philadelphia—1810 Rittenhouse Sq. So.
San Francisco—732 Montgomery St.
KOCH & LOWY
Atlanta—Joe Sherry Assoc., 114 16th St., N.W.
Chicago—1245 Merchandise Mart
Dallas—W. Glenn Hennings, 605 World Trade Ctr.
* Long Island City, NY—21-24 39 Ave., Long Island City, NY 11101, 212/ 786-3520
Los Angeles—Pacific Design Center
Miami—Joe Sherry Assoc., 285 N.W. 71 St.
New York—940 Third Avenue
San Francisco—Joel Bennett, Western Merchandise Mart
KRUPNICK BROS., INC.
Chicago—Hargri, 212 W. Kinzy
Dallas—Gerald Hargett, 220 Decorative Center
Los Angeles—Clark & Burchfield, 100 N. Robertson Blvd.
Miami—74 N.E. 40 St.
New York—979 Third Ave.
Philadelphia—Darr-Luck, The Showplace
San Francisco—Design Products West, 151 Union St.
* Union, N.J.—909 Rahway Ave., Union, NJ 07083, 201/ 687-1400

L

JACK LENOR LARSON, INC.
Atlanta—Jerry Pair & Assoc., 351 Peachtree Hills Ave., N.E.
Boston—George & Frances Davison, 420 Boylston Street
Chicago—Jack Lenor Larsen, Inc., 6-140 Merchandise Mart
Dallas—Walter Lee Culp Assoc., 119 Oak Lawn Plaza
Los Angeles—Jack Lenor Larsen, Pacific Design Center
Miami—Jerry Pair & Assoc., 105 N.E. 39 St.
* New York—232 E. 59 St., New York, NY 10022, 212/ 674-3993
Philadelphia—Duncan & Huggins, 1704 Walnut St.
San Francisco—Kneedler-Fauchere, 101 Kansas St., Space 170
ERIC LAUREN, 964 Third Ave., New York, NY 10022, 212/ 593-3377
ARTHUR H. LEE & JOFA, INC.
Atlanta—Curran Associates, 351 Peachtree Hills Ave., N.E.
Boston—Fortune, Inc., 420 Boylston Street
Chicago—Lee-Larsen, 6-140 Mdse. Mart
Dallas—David L. Shead, Inc., 620 Decorative Center
Los Angeles—Pacific Design Center
* New York—979 Third Ave., New York, NY 10022, 212/ 889-3900
Philadelphia—Paul Klinefelter, Inc., 2400 Market St.

San Francisco—McCune Showroom, 425 Jackson Square

BARBARA LEE ASSOC.
* Miami—3600 N.E. Second Ave., Miami, FL 33137, 305/ 573-1808
New York—Cavallon Associates, 979 Third Ave.

LIGHT/INC., 417 Bleecker St., New York, NY 10014, 212/ 691-3606

LIGHTING ASSOCIATES, INC., 305 E. 63 St., New York, NY 10021, 212/ 751-0515

LIQUID SLEEP INTERIORS, 7119 Melrose Ave., Los Angeles, CA 90046, 213/ 930-1475

M

MALLIN COMPANY
Chicago—Amer. Furn. Mart, 666 Lake Shore Dr.
Dallas—World Trade Center, 2100 Stemmons Freeway
* Los Angeles—2335 E. 27 St., Los Angeles, CA 90058, 213/ 589-6591
Showroom—L.A. Home Furn. Mart, 1933 S. Broadway
San Francisco—Western Merchandise Mart, Mart #2, Suite 120, 875 Stevenson St.

MANUSCREENS, 979 Third Ave., New York, NY 10022, 212/ 421-1270

MARDEN MFG., INC.
* Chicago—5823 N. Ravenswood, Chicago, IL 60660, 312/ 769-5100
Showroom—Marden, 1700 Merchandise Mart
New York—Robert Krellman & Assoc., Inc., 231 E. 55 St.

MARGOWEN, INC.
Dallas—Eliot & Associates, 709 Oak Lawn Plaza
Los Angeles—Jay Clark, 110 S. Robertson Blvd.
* New York—979 Third Ave., New York, NY 10022, 212/ 355-1686
San Francisco—John W. Ledford, Inc., 101 Kansas St., Galleria 240

THE MARKETPLACE, 2400 Market St., Philadelphia, PA 19103, 215/ 561-5000

JOHN MASCHERONI, INC., 979 Third Ave., New York, NY 10022, 212/ 753-9166

MASONITE CORPORATION, 29 N. Wacker Dr., Chicago, IL 60606, 312/ 372-5642

ANDRE MATENCIOT CO., 240 E. 58 St., New York, NY 10022, 212/ 486-9064

MEADOWCRAFT–BIRMINGHAM ORNAMENTAL IRON CO.
* Birmingham, AL—P.O. Box 1357, Birmingham, AL 35201, 205/ 853-2220
Chicago—17-105 Mdse Mart
Dallas—247 Dallas Home Furn. Mart 2000 Stemmons Freeway
High Point—380 Southern Exposition Bldg., Green Dr. Addition
Los Angeles—L.A. Home Furn. Mart, 1933 S. Broadway, Space 722

MIDDLE EAST RUG CORP.
276 Fifth Ave., New York, NY 10001, 212/ 684-5340

CHARLES MINNÉ ROMAN SHADE CO., 8203 Melrose Ave., Los Angeles, CA 90046, 213/ 653-4304

BOB MITCHELL DESIGNS
Atlanta—Vicrtex Sales Div., 1149 Logan Circle, N.W.
Chicago—Crane Wallcoverings, 2335 W. Wabansia
* Culver City, CA—P.O. Box 831, Culver City, CA 90230, 213/ 871-0860
Dallas—Vicrtex Sales Div., 8383 Stemmons Freeway
Los Angeles—Mitchell/Mann, 8687 Melrose Ave., Suite 659
New York—Vicrtex Sales Div., 964 Third Ave.
San Francisco—Vicrtex Sales Div., 101 Kansas Street

MODERN MASTER TAPESTRIES, INC.
Atlanta—Aronson Gallery, 3136 Habersham Rd., N.W.
Boston—Harcus, Krakow, Rosen, Sonnabend Gallery, 7 Newbury St.
Chicago—Hokin Gallery, 200 E. Ontario St.
Los Angeles—Dalzell-Hatfield Galleries Ambassador Hotel, Ambassador Sta. Box 130
* New York—11 E. 57 St., New York, NY 10022, 212/ 838-0413
Showroom—Atelier Int'l, 139 E. 57 St.
San Francisco—ADI, 530 McAllister St.

A. MORJIKIAN
Atlanta—Ernest Gaspard & Assoc., 351 Peachtree Hills Ave., N.E.
Chicago—Watson Smith, 6-127 Mdse Mart

Dallas—E. C. Dicken, Inc., 480 Decorative Center
* New York—150 E. 58 St., New York NY 10022, 212/ 753-8695
San Francisco—L'Armoire, Ghiradell Square, 900 N. Point

N

NATIONAL FLOOR PRODUCTS CO INC.
Atlanta—12 B-7 Atlanta Mdse Mart
Chicago—Nafco, 1310 Mdse Mart
* Florence, AL—P.O. Box 354, Florence AL 35630, 205/ 766-0234
Los Angeles—Nafco, Space 343, Mds Mart, 1933 S. Broadway
New York—Nafco, 919 Third Ave.

NESLE, INC.
Los Angeles—Donghia, Inc., 8715 Melrose Ave.
Miami—LaVerne Gallery, 3925 N. Miami Ave.
* New York—151 E. 57 St., New York, NY 10022, 212/ 755-0515

NESSEN LAMPS, INC.
Atlanta—Friend-Stewart Assoc., 770 Spring St., N.W.
Boston—Leonard Hecker Assoc., Inc., 420 Boylston St.
* Bronx, NY—3200 Jerome Ave., Bronx, NY 10468, 212/ 295-0220
Chicago—1224A Mdse Mart
Los Angeles—C. J. Welch, Inc., 8807 Beverly Blvd.
Miami—Jos Schmidt Co., 3910 N.E. 1st Ave.
New York—315 E. 62 St.
San Francisco—C. J. Welch, Inc., 101 Kansas St.

NETTLE CREEK INDUSTRIES
Chicago—1376 Mdse Mart
Dallas—1054 Trade Mart
* New York—95 Madison Ave., New York, NY 10016, 212/ 683-8781

NEW YORK FURNITURE EXCHANGE, 200 Lexington Ave., New York, NY 10016, 212/ 679-9500

NEW YORK MERCHANDISE MART, 41 Madison Ave., New York, NY 10010, 212/ 889-6540

NIKOVA, INC., 527 Madison Ave., New York, NY 10022, 212/ 758-3440

NORIK, THE ORIENTAL RUG AGENCY, 309 Fifth Ave., New York, NY 10016, 212/ 684-1845

O

ODENHEIMER & BAKER, INC.
Atlanta—Rob't Kelly & Assocs., 351 Peachtree Hills Ave., N.E.
Chicago—The Jack Denst Designs, Inc., 6-117 Mdse Mart
Dallas—David L. Shead, Inc., 620 Decorative Center
* Los Angeles—137 N. Robertson Blvd., Los Angeles, CA 90048, 213/ 271-9183
Miami—Carousel Designs, Inc., 35 N.E. 40 St.
New York—Winfield Design Assoc., 979 Third Ave.
Philadelphia—Rodal Design Collection, Marketplace Space 104

OHLINE CORP.
* Gardena, CA—1930 W. 139 St., Gardena, CA 90249, 213/ 770-0760
Los Angeles—Pacific Design Center

MICHAEL OHNMACHT STAINED GLASS STUDIO, P.O. Box 1172, Aspen, CO 81611, 303/ 925-3134

OLD WORLD MOULDING & FINISHING, INC., 115 Allen Blvd., Farmingdale, NY 11735, 516/ 822-2280

OLYMPUS GRAPHICUS, INC.
Atlanta—Joe Sherry Assocs., 114 16 St., N.W.
* Bainbridge Island, WA—10070 Ferry Terminal, Bainbridge Island, WA 98110, 206/ 623-7700
Chicago—1795 Merchandise Mart
Dallas—Ginger Miceli Assocs., 545 Oak Lawn Plaza
Los Angeles—Fred Graff & Assocs., Showroom 1052, 1933 S. Broadway
Miami—Joe Sherry & Assocs., 285 N.W. 71 St.
New York—Robert Benjamin, 306 E. 61 St.
San Francisco—Brandt Brereton, Etc., #424 Design Center, 101 Kansas St.

ORLINER STUDIOS, 1100 E. Mt. Airy Ave., Philadelphia, PA 19150, 215/ 242-8633

P

THE PACE COLLECTION, INC.
Chicago—1200 Merchandise Mart

Dallas—John Edward Hughes, Inc., 100 Oak Lawn Plaza
Los Angeles—8936 Beverly Blvd.
Miami—47 N.E. 36 St.
* New York—321 E. 62 St., New York, NY 10021, 212/ 838-0331
San Francisco—Nevins-Pearson Assocs., The Icehouse, 151 Union St.

HUBERT PALEY STUDIO, 100 Fifth Avenue, New York, NY 10011, 212/ 691-3355

PANTA-ASTOR
Atlanta—Reed, 673 Ethel St.
Chicago—Crane, 2335 Wabansia Ave.
Dallas—Rosco, 1215 Viceroy Dr.
High Point—Reed, 4617 E. Ind. Ave., Charlotte, N.C.
Miami—Reed, 4100 N.W. 2nd Ave.
New York—Washington Wallpapers, 5015 New Utrecht Ave.
* So. Kearny, NJ—85 Lincoln Hwy., So. Kearny, NJ 07032, 201/ 344-1371

PAISLEY & FRIENDS, 1506 Whitesboro St., Utica, NY 13502, 315/ 732-8262

PATCRAFT MILLS, INC.
Atlanta—13A6, Merchandise Mart
Chicago—1038 Mdse Mart
Dallas—World Trade Center #345
* Dalton, GA—P.O. Box 1087, Industrial Blvd., Dalton, GA 30720, 404/ 278-2134
New York—919 Third Ave., 14th Fl.

NORMAN PERRY, INC.
Atlanta—Ernest Gaspard & Assoc., 351 Peachtree Hills Ave., N.E.
Boston—Berkeley House, 420 Boylston Street
Chicago—Erwin-Lambeth, Inc., 6130 Mdse Mart
Dallas—David Northrop & Co., 212 World Trade Center
Los Angeles—Felice Young & Assoc., 2354 Roscomare Rd.
New York—Chas. W. Yearsley, 214 E. 52nd St., and R. G. Schnoor. Inc., Suite 223, 225 5 Ave.
Philadelphia—Darr-Luck Assoc., 2400 Market St.
* Plymouth, NH—Box 90, Plymouth, NH 03264, 603/ 536-2064

PHILADELPHIA CARPET CO.
Atlanta—Crawford & Thompson, Inc., 1159 Logan Circle, N.W.
* Cartersville, GA—Cartersville, GA 30120, 404/ 382-5200
Chicago—1800 Mdse Mart
Dallas—3402 Dallas Trade Mart
New York—919 Third Ave.
Philadelphia—Allegheny Ave. & C St.
San Francisco—400 Western Furn. Mart, 1355 Market St.

PHOENIX CARPET CO., INC. 979 Third Ave., New York, NY 10022, 212/ 758-5070

PILLOWED FURNITURE & CREATIONS LTD., 9733 Wilshire Blvd., Beverly Hills, CA 90212, 213/ 273-3204

PLASTIC VIEW TRANSPARENT SHADES, INC., 15408 Cabrito, Van Nuys, CA 91400, 213/ 786-2801

PLEXABILITY LTD., 26 E. 21 St., New York, NY 10010, 212/ 677-3450

PORTICO, 201 E. 56 St., New York, NY 10022, 212/ 838-3220

POULIOT DESIGNS CORP., 7400 W. 125 St., Savage, MN 55378, 612/ 890-8144

POSTER AMERICA, 174 Ninth Ave., New York, NY 10011, 212/ 691-1615

Q

QUADRILLE WALLPAPERS & FABRICS
Atlanta—Ernest Gaspard, 351 Peachtree Hills Ave., N.E.
Chicago—John Strauss Showroom, 160 E. Erie St.
Dallas—John Edward Hughes, 118 Oak Lawn Plaza
Los Angeles—Donghia, Inc., 8715 Melrose Ave.
Miami—Atrium, 50 N.E. 40 St.
* New York—979 Third Ave., New York, NY 10022, 212/ 753-2995
Philadelphia—JW Showroom, 1606 Walnut St.
San Francisco—Austin Ellie, 151 Union St.

R

REED WALLCOVERING
* Atlanta—550 Pharr Rd., Suite 300, Atlanta, GA 30305, 404/ 261-6383
Showroom—Chatherene Woods, 87 W. Paces Ferry Rd.
Boston—Reed/WHS Lloyd Wallcoverings, 241 "A" Street

Dallas—Del Risinger, 1625 Stemmons Freeway
Miami—Peggy Lietch, 4029 N. Miami Ave.
New York—Cliff Murvine, WHS Lloyd, 979 Third Ave.

JOSEPH RICHTER, INC.
Chicago—Michael Roberts, Inc., 325 N. Wells St.
* New York—249 E. 57 St., New York, NY 10022, 212/ 755-6094

ROSELINE PRODUCTS. INC., 120 Schmitt Blvd., Farmingdale, NY 11735, 516/ 751-7988

S

SASON CUSTOM CREATIONS, LTD., 195 Chrystie St., New York, NY 10002, 212/ 533-2879

SAXONY CARPET COMPANY, INC.
Atlanta—Threlkeld-Schlemon Assocs., Ltd., 351 Peachtree Hills Ave., N.E.
Boston—Studio Three, 420 Boylston Street
Chicago—Michael Roberts Collection, 325 N. Wells St.
Dallas—Sylvan Garrett Design III, Inc., 580 Oak Lawn Plaza
Los Angeles—Mitchell-Mann Assocs., 8687 Melrose Ave.
* New York—979 Third Ave., New York, NY 10022, 212/ 755-7100
Philadelphia—Maen Showroom Ltd., 2400 Market St.

SCALAMANDRE
Atlanta—351 Peachtree Hills Ave., N.E.
Boston—420 Boylston Street
Chicago—610 Merchandise Mart
Dallas—630 Decorative Center
Los Angeles—131 N. Robertson Blvd.
* New York—950 Third Ave., New York, NY 10022, 212/ 361-8500
Philadelphia—2400 Market St.
San Francisco—615 Sansom St.

F. SCHUMACHER & CO.
Atlanta—Howard Bode, 351 Peachtree Hills Ave., N.E.
Boston—420 Boylston St.
Chicago—Robert Shea, 6-133 Mdse Mart
Dallas—George Santa Cruz, 640 Decorative Center
Los Angeles—Warren Rose, 116 N. Robertson Blvd.
Miami—Marion A. Hoffman, 40 N.E. 40 St.
' New York—939 Third Ave., New York, NY 10022, 212/644-5943
Philadelphia—Robert J. Wolfe, 2400 Market St.
San Francisco—Culmer C. Benton, 101 Kansas St.

I. SCHWARTZ GLASS & MIRROR CO., 412 E. 59 St., New York, NY 10022, 212/759-7866

THE SCULPTURE STUDIO, INC., 202 E. 77 St., New York, NY 10021, 212/ 861-8480

SHARIAN, INC., 368 W. Ponce de Leon Ave., Decatur, GA 30030, 404/373-2274

JOE SHERRY ASSOCIATES, INC.
Atlanta—114 16th St., N.W.
* Miami—285 N.W. 71 St., Miami, FL 33150, 305/757-0659

THE SHOWPLACE, 2 Kansas St., San Francisco, CA 94103, 415/864-1500

SHOWROOM III/HAITIAN COTTON
Chicago—Colie and Harris, Inc., 6-158 Mdse Mart
Dallas—Doak Stowe & Co., 620 Decorative Center
Los Angeles—Kneedler-Fauchere, Pacific Design Center #600
Miami—Bob Collins, Inc., 120 N.E. 39 St.
New York—Thomas K. Smith, 979 Third Ave.
* San Francisco—30 Hotaling Place, Jackson Square, San Francisco, CA 94111, 415/421-8922

SHOWROOM III/YORK COUNTY FURNITURE
Atlanta—Paul B. Raulet, Atlanta Decorative Center
Chicago—Colie and Harris, Inc., 6-158 Mdse Mart
Dallas—E. C. Dicken, Inc., 480 Decorative Center
Los Angeles—Kneedler-Fauchere, Pacific Design Center #600
* San Francisco—30 Hotaling Place, Jackson Square, San Francisco, CA 94111, 415/421-8922

SIEBERTS, COX & L'HERISSON, INC., 101 Kansas St., San Francisco, CA 94131, 415/864-6898

SIESTA BEDDING CO.
* Los Angeles—2223 E. 37 St., Los Angeles, CA 90058, 213/ 583-4571
Showroom—Space 1153-1154 L.A. Home Furn. Mart

San Francisco—Space 690-692, Western Mdse Mart

SIGNATURE FLOORS, INC.
Miami—3841 N.E. Second Ave.
* New York—979 Third Ave., New York, NY 10022, 212/759-1830
San Francisco—Design Products West, 101 Kansas St.

SMITH & WATSON
Atlanta—Ernest Gaspard & Assoc., 351 Peachtree Hills Ave., N.E.
Boston—E. Wells McLean, Inc., 420 Boylston Street
Chicago—Patterson, Flynn & Martin, 1226 Mdse Mart
Dallas—John Edward Hughes, Inc., 100 Oak Lawn Plaza
Los Angeles—The Madsen Co., 8784 Beverly Blvd.
* New York—Dec. Arts Center, 305 E. 63 St., New York, NY 10021, 212/ 355-5615
San Francisco—McCure, 425 Jackson Square

SOUTHEAST WHOLESALE FURNITURE CO., 1065 Williams St., N.W., P.O. Box 7908, Atlanta, GA 30309, 404/ 875-5381

STACY VERTICAL BLINDS, INC., 14832 Schaefer Highway, Detroit, MI 48227, 313/491-2200

STARK CARPET CORP.
Boston—M-Geough Robinson, Inc., 420 Boylston Street
Chicago—1368 Mdse Mart
Dallas—111 Oak Lawn Plaza
Los Angeles—Pacific Des. Ctr., 8687 Melrose Ave.
Miami—161 N.E. 40 St.
* New York—979 Third Ave., New York, NY 10022, 212/752-9000

STATE PAVILION, 964 Third Ave., New York, NY 10022, 212/935-1030

STENDIG, INC.
Atlanta—MacKerer, Walker, Graham, Inc., 19 14 St., N.W.
Boston—Marcia Campbell, 815 E. Broadway, So. Boston
Chicago—Stendig, 1158 Mdse Mart
Los Angeles—Stendig, 8919 Beverly Blvd.
Miami—MacKerer, Walker, Graham, Inc., 276 N.E. 67 St.
* New York—410 E. 62 St., New York, NY 10021, 212/838-6050
San Francisco—Space 210, 151 Union St.

STILNOVO IMPORTS, INC.
Miami—Barbara Lee Assoc., Inc., 3600 N.E. 2nd Ave.
* New York—215 Lexington Ave., Suite 806, New York, NY 10016, 212/684-0790
Philadelphia—The Marketplace, 2400 Market St.

STROHEIM & ROMANN
Boston—420 Boylston Street
Chicago—6148 Mdse Mart
Dallas—2615 Fairmount St.
Los Angeles—133 N. Robertson Blvd.
Miami—119 N.E. 39 St.
* New York—155 E. 56 St., New York, NY 10022, 212/ 691-0700
Philadelphia—2400 Market St.
San Francisco—445 Jackson St.

JOHN STUART INC./JOHN WIDDICOMB CO.
Boston—90 Berkeley Street
Chicago—6-17 Merchandise Mart
* New York—205 E. 58 St., New York, NY 10022, 212/ 421-1200
Philadelphia—2301 Chestnut St.

SWAN BRASS BEDS, 1955 E. 16 St., Los Angeles. CA 90021, 213/748-5315

SWIVELIER CO., INC., 33 Route 304, Nanuet, NY 10954, 914/623-3471

T

TELESCOPE FOLDING FURNITURE CO., INC.
Atlanta—Atlanta Mdse Mart, Space 1602
Chicago—American Mart, Space 1719-20, Lake Shore Dr.
* Granville, NY—Church St., Granville, NY 12832, 518/642-1100
High Point—Southern Furn. Market Ctr., Space 410-412
New York—New York Furniture Exchange, 192 Lexington Ave.
San Francisco—Western Mdse Mart, Space 664-666

RICHARD E. THIBAUT, INC.
Atlanta—Seabrook Wallcoverings, 351 Peachtree Hills Ave., N.E.
Chicago—Thybony Wallcoverings, 620 Mdse Mart
Dallas—Seabrook Wallcoverings, 180 Decorative Center
Los Angeles—Kinney Wallcoverings, 111 S. Robertson Blvd.
Miami—Seabrook Wallcoverings, 4330 N.E. Second Ave.
* New York—315 Fifth Ave., New York, NY 10016, 212/686-0086
Showroom—Thibaut Wallcoverings, 204-206 E. 58 St.
San Francisco—Kinney Brothers, 875 Stevenson St.

ERNEST TREGANOWAN, INC., 306 E. 61 St., New York, NY 10021, 212/755-1050

TRI-MARK DESIGNS
Atlanta—Modern Assocs., 1178 W. Peachtree St., N.W.
Chicago—InterGroup Collection Ltd., 1209 Mdse Mart
Dallas—Martin & Wright, 200 Oak Lawn Plaza
Los Angeles—Rockwell-West, 528 Pacific Design Center
Miami—39 East, 90 N.E. 39 St.
New York—Quantum Designs, Inc., 979 Third Ave.
* Philadelphia—Bilt-Well Showrooms, 1006 Arch St., Philadelphia, PA 19107, 215/923-5971
San Francisco—Cahill-Ruben Ltd., Space 164, 101 Kansas St.

TROPITONE FURNITURE CO., INC.
Chicago—1719 Merchandise Mart
Dallas—No. 212 World Trade Center
* Irvine, CA—17101 Armstrong, Irvine, CA 92714, 714/540-8760
Miami—Joe Sherry Assocs., 285 N.W. 71 St.
New York—The Cavallon Showroom, 979 Third Ave.
San Francisco—KKS & Assocs., 151 Union St.
* Sarasota, FL—P.O. Box 3197, Sarasota, FL 33578, 813/355-2715

TROUVAILLES, INC.
Atlanta—Decorators Walk, 351 Peachtree Hills Ave.
Chicago—Trouvailles, #1221 Mdse Mart
Dallas—Trouvailles, 701 Oak Lawn Plaza
Los Angeles—Mitchell-Mann Assoc., 8687 Melrose Ave.
Miami—Vanleigh Furniture Co., 4100 N.E. Second Ave.
New York—Trouvailles, 305 E. 63 St.
San Francisco—Design Mart, Inc., 151 Union St.
* Watertown, MA—64 Grove St., Watertown, MA 02172, 617/926-2520

TURNER LTD.
Chicago—600 Mdse Mart
Los Angeles—C. J. Welch, Inc., 8807 Beverly Blvd.
Miami—10 N.E. 39 St.
* New York—305 E. 63 St., New York, NY 10021, 212/758-4744
San Francisco—CDI, 315 Pacific Ave.

U

UNIKA-VAEV USA, INC.
Boston—ICF, 27 Stanhope Street
Chicago—ICF, 1010 Mdse Mart
Los Angeles—ICF, 8899 Beverly Blvd.
* New York—ICF, 145 E. 57 St., New York, NY 10022, 212/752-5870
San Francisco—ICF, 151 Union St.

V

VANLEIGH FURNITURE SHOWROOMS, INC.
Atlanta—Vanleigh Furniture, 525 Plaster Ave., N.E.
Miami—Vanleigh Furniture Showrooms, 4100 N.E. 2nd Ave.
* New York—323 E. 44 St. New York, NY 10017, 212/684-6700

ALBERT VAN LUIT & CO.
Chicago—6/154 Merchandise Mart
* Los Angeles—4000 Chevy Chase Dr., Los Angeles, CA 90039, 213/245-5106
Showroom—8687 Melrose Ave., Space 625
New York—979 Third Avenue
San Francisco—101 Kansas St., Space 133

VINTAGE HOUSE, INC., 1254 Montgomery Ave., San Bruno, CA 94066, 415/ 589-1100

VIRGINIA METALCRAFTERS, INC.
Atlanta—Whitlow-Ringdahl, 9C1 Atlanta Mdse Mart
Boston—Paul B. Janssen, Ltd., Bedford, Room 160, The Center
Chicago—W. C. Owen, Inc., 1520-21 Mdse Mart
Dallas—Jack Housman, Inc., 2101 Dallas Trade Mart
High Point—Whitlow-Ringdahl, 282 Southern Furn. Bldg.
Los Angeles—Dave Gross & Assoc., 649 S. Olive St.
New York—Room 501, 225 5 Ave.

* Waynesboro, VA—1010 E. Main St., Waynesboro, VA 22980, 703/ 942-8205

V'SOSKE
Chicago—E. Virginia Kemper & Assoc., 6-127 Mdse Mart
Dallas—Pedlar & Co., 2611 Fairmount
Los Angeles—Douglas V'Soske, 9020 Beverly Blvd.
Miami—Bob Collins, Inc., 120 N.E. 39 St.
* New York—Lord & Adams, Inc., 155 E. 56 St., New York, NY 10022, 212/ 688-1150
San Francisco—John W. Ledford, 101 Kansas St.

W

SHERLE WAGNER INTERNATIONAL
Atlanta—Paul B. Raulet, Inc., 351 Peachtree Hills Ave., N.E.
Chicago—S. J. Campbell Co., 1248 Mdse Mart
Dallas—John Edward Hughes, Inc., 1444 Oak Lawn Ave.
Los Angeles—Kneedler-Fauchere, 8687 Melrose Ave.
* New York—60 E. 57 St., New York, NY 10022, 212/ 758-3300
San Francisco—Kneedler-Fauchere, 101 Kansas St.

WALKER MANUFACTURING CO., 408 Pacific Design Center, 8687 Melrose Ave., Los Angeles, CA 90069, 213/ 659-1718

WEAVERS DOMAIN LTD./WINDOW MODES, INC.
Chicago—Michael Roberts, Inc., 325 N. Wells St.
Dallas—Walter Lee Culp Assocs., 1444 Oak Lawn Plaza
Los Angeles—Decorators Walk, 131 N. Robertson Ave.
Miami—S. G. K. Decorators of Florida, 130 N.E. 40 St.
* New York—S. G. K. Decorators, Inc., 979 Third Ave., New York, NY 10022, 212/ 355-7763
San Francisco—Decorators Walk, 101 Kansas St.

WHITE FURNITURE CO., Box 367, Mebane, NC 27302, 919/ 563-1217

THE WICKER WORKS, 650 Potrero Ave., San Francisco, CA 94110, 415/ 285 3496

WINDOW WORKS UNLIMITED, 979 Third Ave., New York, NY 10022, 212/ 832-2250

WOOD AND HOGAN, INC.
Dallas—Gerald Hargett, Inc., 220 Decorative Ctr.
* New York—305 E. 63 St., New York, NY 10021, 212/ 355-1335

THE WRECKING BAR OF ATLANTA, INC., 292 Moreland Ave., N.E., Atlanta, GA 30307, 404/ 525-0468

The Baker Collector's Edition is a selection of reproductions which exemplify the enduring qualities of outstanding early design: proportion, detail, finish and material. Each is meticulously reproduced in the 18th century tradition of skilled hand-craftsmanship.

For example, the swan neck pediment of our Georgian mahogany secretary is

intricately pierced in the manner of the original. On each of the five drawer fronts of the William and Mary chest, inlays and bandings surround rare French walnut veneers. Both the knee and foot of the Chippendale cabriole chair leg are deeply carved.

You are invited to see the entire Baker collection in any of the showrooms listed below.

Baker
Knapp & Tubbs

Distinguished manufacturer and distributor with showrooms in Atlanta, Chicago, Cleveland, Dallas, Grand Rapids, High Point, Houston, Los Angeles, Miami, New York, Philadelphia, San Francisco.

BELGIAN LINEN WALLCOVERING

Timeless Belgian linen, nature's own fiber. Flax is harvested, processed, spun, and finally woven by Belgian craftsmen into unique linen wallcoverings and fabrics. Elegant textures, luxurious patterns, superb weaves, rich natural colorations—all attributes of Belgian linen. Can be treated to meet with flame resistance standards, are easily installed, require minimum maintenance, and withstand wear and tear.

For additional information: **Belgian Linen Association, 280 Madison Avenue, New York, N.Y. 10016**

WATER MUSIC BY WAGNER

Yes. We know. We know. In the first place Wagner didn't write Water Music. It was Handel. In the second place Wagner's first name was Richard. This Wagner is Sherle, and these incredibly beautiful bowls and matching fixtures are just a few of his variations on a theme. His other compositions are equally original.

60 EAST 57TH STREET, NEW YORK, **SHERLE WAGNER** NEW YORK, 10022, PLAZA 8-3300

A New York apartment.

Good taste in decorating is within everyone's budget and so are the services of a good designer. The benefit of our professional skills can save you unnecessary expenditures.

Residential Interiors by

EVERETT BROWN ASSOCIATES

225 East 57th Street • New York, New York • (212) PLAZA 5-1332

The original Berberwool landscape artists.

The Eurotex Berberwool Collection of carpets and wallcoverings are expressly designed for homes where quality, elegance, and simplicity are more important than price. (The average living room begins at $900.)

Available through your architect or designer. Or call Eurotex at 215-LO8-4300 for the name of the fine store in your city.

EUROTEX
The Marketplace
2400 Market Street Philadelphia, PA 19103

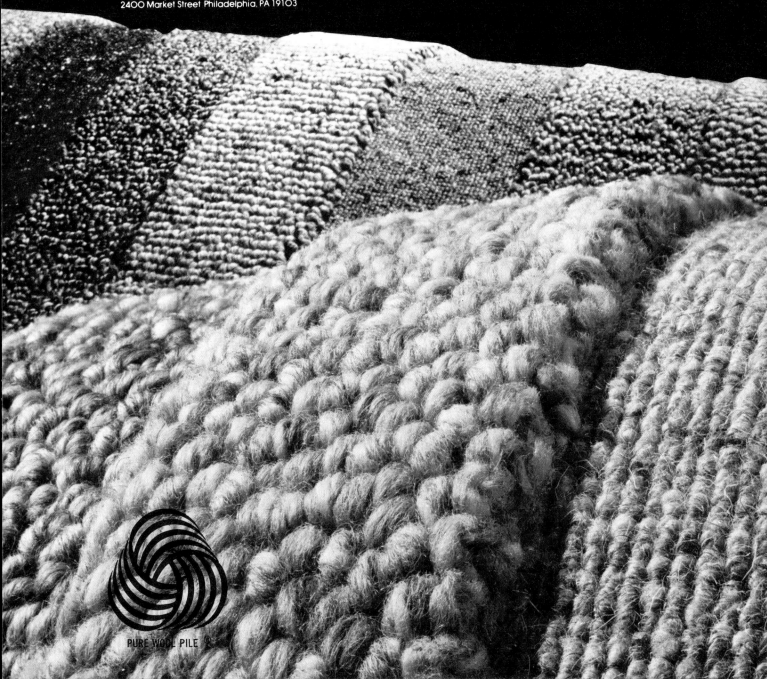

PURE WOOL PILE

ARCHITECTURE & DESIGN

New Books

200 YEARS OF AMERICAN ARCHITECTURAL DRAWING

By David Gebhard and Deborah Nevins. A fully illustrated appraisal of American architectural drawing — the first of its kind. A scholarly study of 85 distinguished architects, the text covers the entire range of architectural drawing (including formalized presentation sketches, working drawings, etc.), their purposes, and their relationship to "high art" within the framework of 19th and 20th century history. Among those included are Thomas Jefferson, John Trumbull, Calvert Vaux, Henry Hobson Richardson, Louis Henry Sullivan, Ludwig Mies van der Rohe, Frank Lloyd Wright, Louis I. Kahn, Paul Rudolph, Eero Saarinen, Robert Venturi — and 74 others. 304 pp. 9 x 12. 250 b/w illus. Notes. Bibl. Index. ISBN 0-8230-7470-6 CIP. $30.00 (May 15)

FOR PEDESTRIANS ONLY:
Planning, Design, and Management of Traffic-Free Zones

By Roberto Brambilla and Gianni Longo. With a Foreword by Bernard Rudofsky. This in-depth summary and analysis of traffic-free zoning in European and North American cities has long been needed as a guide on how to make cities more habitable — free from noise, pollution, and the turmoil of traffic. After discussing objectives, the authors examine strategies for involving the community, promoting legislation and financing, design of public spaces, and implementation. There are twenty case studies as well as a compendium of over 70 American pedestrian malls. 208 pp. 8¼ x 11. 250 b/w illus. Notes. Appendix. Bibl. Index. ISBN: 0-8230-7174-X. CIP. $24.95 (April 15)

WOMEN IN AMERICAN ARCHITECTURE:
A Historic and Contemporary Perspective

Edited by Susana Torre. with a foreword by Marita O-Hare. "Absorbing reading," says the *New York Times* of this unique survey of women's role in the American architectural profession. The volume is divided into five parts, with chapters contributed by thirteen women well known in architectural journalism. It includes a pictorial overview of how professional women have designed for and written about women as workers in the home; the varied careers of women architects from the mid-19th century through the 1960s; the position of women as architectural critics; the contemporary perspective of women in the profession; and women's spatial symbolism. 224 pp. 8¼ x 11. 250 b/w illus. Chart. Notes. Bibl. Biog. notes. Index. ISBN: 0-8230-7485-4. CIP. $25.00

Recommended Books

FRANK LLOYD WRIGHT'S USONIAN HOUSES: The Case for Organic Architecture By John Sargeant. This eagerly-awaited definitive analysis of Wright's later period, when his genius came to full flower in his Usonian houses, the Taliesin working communities, and his plans for Broadacre City, offers a well-documented overview of the master's achievements. "John Sargeant has compiled . . . a creditable array of material that is more than of passing interest." — *Architectural Record*. 208 pp. 9 x 10. 125 b/w illus. Appendices. Bibl. Index. ISBN 0-8230-7177-4. CIP. $24.50

OUTDOOR SCULPTURE: Object and Environment By Margaret A. Robinette. "An informative, excellent study of large-scaled, modern outdoor sculpture. Outdoor sculpture as public art is here examined in an excellent new book which is well illustrated with 175 black and white illustrations." — *Bulletin*, Garden Center of Cleveland. 192 pp. 8½ x 8½. 175 b/w illus. Appendices. Bibl. Index. ISBN 0-8230-7406-4. CIP. $24.50

A GUIDE TO BUSINESS PRINCIPLES AND PRACTICES FOR INTERIOR DESIGNERS By Harry Siegel. "Meticulously done instructions and examples of usual business forms and recommended procedures. I have never found anything I have gone to this book for . . . to be in error."—*Interior Designers World*. 208 pp. 9 x 12. Over 40 illus. ISBN 0-8230-7251-7. $16.50

NEW USES FOR OLD BUILDINGS By Sherban Cantacuzino. "This book will be of interest for anyone concerned with our cities and their environs, and should be required reading for those professional planners of the 'demolish and rebuild' school. . . . Excellent photographs and plans for each selection."—*Library Journal*. 280 pp. 8¾ x 11¾. 230 line drawings. 520 b/w illus. Index. ISBN 0-8230-7390-4. CIP. $29.95

THE FUTURE OF THE CITY: New Directions in Urban Planning By Peter Wolf. "Valuable — as a handbook for laymen. [What Dr. Wolf] has done is to summarize clearly and concisely exactly where planning thought stands today . . . [The book is] an informed discussion of problems such as housing, transportation, historic preservation and land use."—*The New York Times*. "A solid and serious study of the current state of the American city, how it came about, and its possible future evolution. . . . Reaches beyond the architect and professional planner to the general public, for the book's great virtue lies in its explanation of the revolution that has occurred in planning in the last ten years." — *Progressive Architecture*. 208 pp. 9 x 12. 146 b/w illus. Appendix. Index. ISBN-0-8230-7182-0. CIP. $20.50

NEIGHBORHOOD CONSERVATION: Handbook of Methods and Techniques By Robert H. McNulty and Stephen A. Kliment. "This report is worthwhile for many reasons and warrants our attention. The graphic organization of textual material is superb and the reader is provided with easy reference to places, policies, and issues."—*Journal of the American Institute of Planners*. 256 pp. 10 x 10. 60 b/w illus. Resources List. Index. ISBN 0-8230-7380-7. CIP. $18.95

HISTORIC HOUSES: Restored and Preserved By Marian Page. "From the introductory survey of the four styles [Colonial, Federal, Greek Revival, and Romantic] and the capsule chronology of each house to the specific problems and decisions encountered by the preservation organizations, technical consultants, and history scholars, the book clearly presents the restoration process as a combination of many efforts. The quality of the text is paralleled by the superb illustrations, including photographs of the furnishings . . . interior spaces . . . and exterior."—*Library Journal*. 208 pp. 9 x 12. 200 b/w illus. Bibl. Index. ISBN 0-8230-7275-4. CIP. $25.00

Please write for a complete catalog. **The Whitney Library of Design** 1515 Broadway, New York, N.Y. 10036

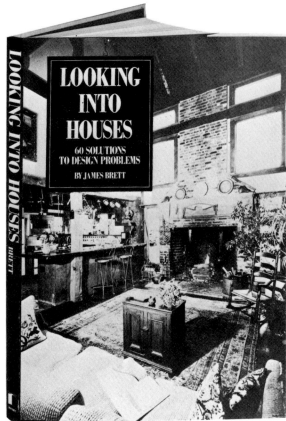

DECORATIVE ELEGANCE is reflected in every detail of this lovely bedroom

On the walls the airy fern pattern is ALSACE which has been combined with the companion pattern METRICO to create this smart background. The bedspread is an ingenious combination of the two patterns and the chair in foreground is upholstered with METRICO. All are available in 5 very distinctive colorways.

THE INITIAL COLLECTION, designed and styled by JOHN LEIGH SPATH . . . available only through interior designers and the design departments of fine stores

Albert **Van Luit & Co.**

WALLCOVERINGS AND RELATED FABRICS

for the

MOST BEAUTIFUL ROOMS

in your home

Send 50¢ for
INITIAL COLLECTION
brochure of beautiful
full color pictures
**4000-AM Chevy Chase Dr.
Los Angeles 90039**